Paths Crossed

HEART SHOTS

The Shocking True Story
of a Dark Day in the
MICHIGAN & INDIANA
STATE POLICE

by

Clif Edwards

Paths Crossed

HEART SHOTS

The Shocking True Story
of a Dark Day in the
MICHIGAN & INDIANA
STATE POLICE

by
CLIF EDWARDS

Copy Edited by William T. Pelletier, Ph.D.

Published by ShowMe Publishing, USA

ISBN – 979-8564488662
Library of Congress Control Number – 2020923459

**In Memory of these Heroes who
Stood in Harm's Way on
September 30, 1957**

~

Trooper Douglas Vogel
Michigan State Police

Trooper Dugald Pellot
Michigan State Police

Sergeant Frederick O'Donnell
Michigan State Police

Trooper William Kellems
Indiana State Police

Trooper Robert Pond
Indiana State Police

Sheriff Charles Dudley
Jennings County, Indiana

Deputy Sheriff Clyde Perkins
Jennings County, Indiana

Patrolman Lester Kenens
North Vernon, Indiana Police Department

Table of Contents

Part C – AFTERMATH

FOREWORD

When the Michigan Law Enforcement Officers Memorial
was dedicated in 2019, it displayed the engraved names of
588 fallen peace officers. Eight of them died while serving in
Lenawee County, a place I consider home. Of those eight, four
were troopers. Of those four troopers, one was murdered.
Drawn to research his murder, I learned that he was not the
only hero and victim on that fateful day.
While all fallen peace officers have a story to be told and a
sacrifice to be remembered, here in this book
I will share the events surrounding and occurring on
September 30, 1957, a dark day in the history of the
Michigan & Indiana State Police.

PART A – AT LARGE

"There is evil in every human heart,
which may remain latent,
perhaps, through the whole life;
but circumstances may rouse it to activity."
~ Nathaniel Hawthorne ~

Chapter I – HOPE

Victor Whitley peered through the prison bars, observing the shadow creep across its yard. Glancing at his wrist, he compared the shadow's line to the hands on his watch. "Yes," he thought, "the days are definitely getting longer." He yearned to see the sunset, but the high wall, topped with menacing razor-wire, prevented that.

Standing at parade rest, something he learned during his short stint in the army, he listened for the courier's shuffling footsteps, footsteps he knew only too well. For more than twenty years this had been his routine, but it felt like forever. He hoped the courier might bring him a particular piece of mail.

Perhaps today he would receive the letter granting him a clemency hearing. He had always been a model inmate, plus he had the benefit of his once court-appointed attorney having risen to be the judge of his motion. And a friend who had oddly evolved from that explosive day had recently come into a position of influence concerning the hearing. He crossed his fingers that his lucky stars were finally aligning.

Feet shoulder-width apart, hands clasped behind his back, and head held motionless, he faced forward and waited. Appearing dull and compliant, Whitley knew himself to be "dumb like a fox." He had often wondered if anyone would ever dig deeper into the events of September 30, 1957. If anyone ever researched and analyzed the events leading up to that tempestuous day and those following, it would make quite a book. He fervently hoped it would never happen – just let it be forgotten.

As he waited, he now tried to practice an empty mind. Three breaths into it his brain echoed, "My finger never touched the trigger until we got on the bridge." He had been thinking and saying this for so long that he had convinced himself it was true. But was it?

With that, his mind drifted back to how it was that he had spent the prime of his life in prison. To anyone watching, he would have appeared to be in a trance.

Growing up poor in Granger, Texas, he was young when his parents divorced. He made it to eleventh grade before dropping out of high school. Many psychologists would have probably said he was at risk. His good looks and quiet personality gained him some grace, providing him an attractive bride for a few years.

After they split, he relocated to the east side of Texas, where he worked with his dad in the oil rigging business, but that ended when his dad refused to pay off his boat debt.

He moved on, joining the army. It wasn't long before he was discharged from Camp Chaffee in Arkansas for bedwetting. He then found employment with a bottling company in Austin, Texas, that is, until he was fired for wrecking one of their trucks. From there he made his way to Maine where his brother was stationed at an Air Force base near Bangor. It wasn't long before he wore out that welcome.

So far, Victor Whitley's life had pretty much been that of a loser. He may have been proud that at age 26 he had never been arrested – as long as you don't count the night he spent in jail for drunkenness. His next path crossed would change that.

Chapter II – MATCHED

Whitley faced north as he walked south. His right arm extended at a near 45-degree angle, thumb up. From his left hand hung his suitcase, which contained everything he owned. It wasn't too heavy. In the distance, emerging from the pavement's heat mirage, a green car was approaching. It was early June 1957, and Maine's tourist season had not yet begun; traffic was sparse.

As the car neared, he recognized it to be a 1954 Chevrolet Bel Air. He could not tell that it was stolen. Staring into the approaching windshield, Whitley strained to make eye contact with its driver as the car smoothly braked to a stop beside him. The driver and sole occupant appeared to be a short man who looked to be about a decade older than himself.

One can imagine the conversations that followed, with the driver saying in his West Virginia accent through the half-open window, "Where you headed?"

Whitley leaning over and answering in a Texas drawl, "Nowhere in particular, but as far south as I can get."

"Hop in, sounds like we're going to the same place." And with that, Whitley squeezed his suitcase into the back and took a seat in the front. Being his nature, Whitley probably said little except to answer the questions posed by the driver as they zoomed south.

Bit by bit, as the miles clicked off, they shared their censored stories. One thing they soon realized that they had in common was that neither had graduated from high school. Whitley learned that the driver's name was Ralph Taylor and that he had recently been paroled from a West Virginia prison. It's doubtful that Taylor disclosed that it was for raping a nine-year-old girl.

As they exhausted small talk, a kinship began to develop, and then silence. While telephone poles flashed by, Taylor pondered approaching Whitley about becoming his partner. He decided to make his play.

Taylor probably pulled a bundle of cash from his pocket for Whitley to see and then asked, "You know how I got this?" And then answering his own question, he lifted his shirttail to expose a pistol tucked in his waistband as he said, "With this."

Taylor's persuasion likely continued by saying that during his prison tenure he had been tutored in the art of armed robbery by the best. It was easy and exciting work that paid well. He said the secret to not getting caught was to have a plan and to know how to be invisible.

By invisible, Taylor said to appear as a law-abiding citizen, never draw attention to yourself by speeding or the like, and immediately leave the state where you had just committed your robbery. It is doubtful he came right out and asked Whitley to join him, but he likely implied it by saying, "It's good to have a trusted partner." He closed his pitch by again pointing to the gun with the fisted cash as he said, "There's no way I'm going back to the pen."

Learning this, Whitley likely became a bit unnerved as he recognized that his chauffeur suffered from little man syndrome. He concealed his nervousness as he pondered Taylor's demeanor and all that he had said. Perhaps Whitley felt solicited.

One can envision that evening found them stopping at one of those combination motel-restaurants along the highway. There Taylor provided the nearly destitute Whitley with food and shelter.

That night, with the effect of Taylor's "Old Taylor" whiskey swirling in his head, Whitley stared at the ceiling from a motel-room bed contemplating what the day had brought before him. Taylor had shared much, and Whitley sensed that come morning, he would have to decide whether to join up with Taylor or separate from him. Taylor's dominating personality was a concern, but Whitley had confidence in his ability as an influencer. Back and forth his thoughts went until finally he drifted off to sleep.

There was much more to Ralph Taylor. Taylor had both married and become a father in 1940. On September 2, 1942, he joined the Army. While he was known to be a good swimmer and diver, his enlistment papers only noted that he had two years of high school, his only skill being that of a driver. Oddly, these papers also listed him as being separated with no dependents. In reality he was married with one, maybe two children at the time.

Taylor was only 5-04 in height and very pigeon-chested, features that had undoubtedly garnered him a lot of teasing as an adolescent. The army, however, recognized the personal toughness these challenges had created and his swimming aptitude. After completion of boot camp, Taylor went on to become a paratrooper. He even became an instructor, training fellow paratroopers on how to survive jumping into the ocean with their gear and then swimming.

As an instructor at the Miami Beach Wartime Training Center in Florida, he became friends with the famous Johnny Weissmuller, an Olympic swimming champion and the original Tarzan. By the time of World War II, Weissmuller was too old to be in the military, but he did help teach ocean swimming to servicemen. His unique style of swimming with his head out of the water had practical application to a soldier's survival in an aquatic environment. On the picture Taylor mailed home, he indicated which swimming soldier was him by writing, "Me."

Ralph Taylor training troops in swimming

Compliments of Sandra Taylor, Ralph Taylor's daughter-in-law

During this time, Taylor's wife and his young son visited him in Miami. It just so happened that Weissmuller's son was the same age as Taylor's. Perhaps this led to Taylor's son Rex getting his first swimming lessons from Tarzan, who he always claimed taught him to swim.

With World War II raging, Taylor's time for overseas duty came. His discharge papers indicate that he was assigned to the 82nd Airborne and served two years, one month, and three days in the Middle East. Pictures he sent home fit that region of the world.

One of the pictures was of Taylor kneeling with two young girls, one holding an infant. On the back of the picture he wrote in cursive, "My two girlfriends age 8 and 9. They don't marry here until they are at least 11. Guess I'll have to wait a couple of years. HaHa. Love Ralph."

Ralph Taylor posing with "girlfriends" in Middle East

Compliments of Sandra Taylor, Ralph Taylor's daughter-in-law

What action Taylor saw or participated in remains a mystery. He survived the war to receive an honorable discharge at the rank of corporal on September 28, 1945. It is interesting to note that his discharge papers indicate he was also awarded an EAME (Europe-Africa-Middle East) Ribbon, a Good Conduct Ribbon, and that his military occupational specialty was "Athletic Inst 283." He only held a Sharpshooter marksmanship rating, which is considered mediocre by most.

Within a year of Taylor being discharged from the military, his wife, now with three children, separated from him. This was about the same time that he was convicted of the rape of a nine-year-old girl and sent to a West Virginia prison where he would serve ten years.

Disowned by his wife, but not divorced, Taylor was paroled from prison on February 6, 1957, to live with his sister Rena in Saint Albans, West Virginia. While ten years is a long time, people of the county had not forgotten what he had done. Shunned by most, he stayed with his sister only a few months before disappearing.

It wasn't until May 7, 1957, that the parole board declared Taylor a parole violator. It's unclear why they listed him as armed and dangerous; perhaps it was his volatile personality and military experience.

Ironically, that was the same day the Chevrolet that Taylor and Whitley now rode in was reported stolen in Portsmouth, Ohio. Taylor could not know his good fortune, namely that an error had been made in reporting the serial number of the stolen Chevrolet to the police. This mistake would make it difficult for officers to detect that the Chevrolet was stolen. It is interesting that Saint Albans and Portsmouth are only 80 miles apart.

During his prison stint, Taylor had undoubtedly been coached on how to be a criminal. It would appear that he took a particular interest in armed robbery. Coupled with his military training, it was a discipline he had perfected and, until now, had practiced alone.

Even if Whitley had known all these things, it is doubtful it would have made a difference in his decision to join up with Taylor. Whitley had tried many conventional means to get along in society and had failed, humiliated time after time. Now before him was a doorway to an utterly different path.

The next morning, rested, showered, and fed, Whitley decided to pursue what Taylor had implied, becoming his partner in crime. He hoped that his influencing personality would mesh well with Taylor's dominating one. His new course was not merely unconventional but illegal, not merely illegal but dangerous. Come what might, until then he would live the good life.

Together, they were matched.

Chapter III – ROBBERS

One wonders who Taylor and Whitley's childhood heroes were. Were they John Dillinger, Bonnie & Clyde, and the like? In studying the numerous robberies the duo committed leading to September 30, 1957, and the events of that day, one has to agree with a statement that Whitley later made, "We weren't petty thieves."

Like military units with standing orders, they appeared to have developed rules they followed, contingency plans for a worst-case scenario, and loyalties till death do they part. Like the police they would encounter, they too were trained, but their rules of engagement did not have to be legal.

Perhaps taking a lesson from their heroes, they never robbed a bank. Banks were FDIC insured, which made robbing one a federal offense and would draw the FBI into the investigation, something to be avoided. The FBI would look nationwide for similar crimes and methods of operation.

Second, they almost never consecutively hit the same state. In fact, most often they had a spacer state between robberies. This made it difficult for the state authorities to recognize a pattern and to pool clues, leads, and evidence. This method of operation kept them under the police radar, so to speak.

They agreed on each other's role and they stayed with the script unless contingency plans had to be implemented. Taylor brandished the gun and made the demands. Also armed, Whitley's primary task was to bind and gag the victims. They prepared binding kits, consisting of four-foot lengths of clothesline, one-inch adhesive tape, and gags from tissue that they kept in zippered shaving kits.

But first, before Whitley could be a robber, he needed a gun. On

June 6, 1957, the newly matched duo patronized the Mountaineer Sport Shop in Morgantown, West Virginia. There Whitley selected a .32 caliber Mauser as his pistol of choice. Taylor, now wanting to carry three guns, added a .32 caliber Colt to his armament of a .44 Smith & Wesson and a .380 Savage.

One wonders where they trained with the pistols. But they must have done so, as a day would come when they would demonstrate their marksmanship. With Taylor's military background, it is likely he took the lead on this. Having only qualified as a sharpshooter in the army, Taylor would not be considered an expert shooter. But Taylor's challenges in life had taught him to adapt, improvise, and overcome. He would compensate for his mediocre shooting ability by luring his target close before firing. Perhaps he subscribed to the adage, "Don't fire until you see the whites of their eyes."

It was still June when Taylor and Whitley committed their first robbery as a team. They cased the business and planned every detail they could imagine. For reasons unknown, the business they chose was a Thom McAn shoe store in Louisville, Kentucky. It went like clockwork. Having made their debut in Kentucky, they were now "off and running."

With new cash in hand and always careful not to draw police attention, they made their way to Arkansas, perhaps enjoying the frivolities that Little Rock had to offer. As their money dwindled, they again looked to replenish it. Going south, their next prey was to be a drug store in El Dorado, Arkansas.

They then bounced north, and once they had crossed into Missouri they resumed the good life until cash again ran low. Their next resupply would come from a liquor store in Kansas City, Missouri, from where they quickly crossed into the state of Kansas. They then leisurely made their way west. It would appear that as they enjoyed their loot, they decided to add to their menu a finance company in Trinidad, Colorado. Finding them more lucrative, Taylor and Whitley soon made finance companies one of their favorite entrées.

It would appear that in Trinidad the credentials of Louis L. Schick, a man similar in age to Whitley, became available for the taking. Recognizing that one day they might need an alias, they stole them. Onward, they would keep an eye out for identification that would be fitting for Taylor.

Apparently, Colorado was far enough west for the duo, and the finance company had provided enough capital for them to double back all the way to Morgantown, West Virginia. There they made their next withdrawal from a Thoroughfare Supermarket.

An observer might ask what was the draw to Morgantown? Was it because it was close to Taylor's home turf, was it spite, or was it some reason only Taylor knew? From that point until what would eventually be their last robbery, they exclusively robbed liquor stores and finance companies.

In July, they hit a liquor store in Texarkana, Arkansas, and then another in Shreveport, Louisiana. They then felt it time to hit their second finance company. This one was in Greenville, South Carolina.

It was late July when they robbed another finance company. This one was on Highway 90 east of New Orleans. Out of character, they then robbed a liquor store in the same state the very next night, albeit it was in northern Louisiana. One might speculate that the cash from the finance company had been minimal, or the liquor store looked especially lucrative. Then on to Chattanooga, Tennessee, followed by Atlanta, Georgia, where they robbed liquor stores in both cities.

Returning to Kentucky, they robbed the Seaboard Finance Company in Covington, once again leaving a man and woman tied up in the backroom with a clothesline. Had anybody been taking notes, they would have realized this was a part of their method of operation in what was an undetected nationwide crime wave.

It was mid-August when they returned to the Northeast, the region where they had been matched. While reconnoitering the ABC Loan Company in Uniontown, Pennsylvania, they finally came across credentials that could support an alias for Taylor, likely stolen from an unlocked car. The credentials were in the name of Cecil R. Compeau, a man but a few years younger than Taylor. These credentials joined those fitting Whitley and were tucked away, to be available at a future date. Making their getaway from the ABC robbery, they motored to Frederick, Maryland, where they hit a liquor store.

With this cluster of states being geographically close together, especially in comparison to the Midwest, they quickly jumped across the line to Delaware where they lay low. As they did, their attention was drawn to the American Finance Company in Wilmington. After casing it, they struck again. According to Whitley, it was from there that they made their record withdrawal of $4000.

Three or four days later they had worked their way back to Kentucky, robbing a finance company in Hopkinsville. From there they crossed the Mississippi River to rob a finance company in Cape Girardeau, Missouri. There they confronted what Whitley described as "a girl," tying her up and stealing $200.

They then re-crossed the "Big Muddy" and traveled to Terre Haute, Indiana. It was Thursday, September 26, 1957, when they robbed Lucy Kern, the clerk at the Household Finance Company, stealing $1000. When her husband, an Indiana trooper, asked her if she was scared, she said, "Not after they tied my legs together."

No one would have predicted that four days later, her husband would be called from bed to man a blockade in hopes of catching the killers of an Indiana trooper and a Michigan trooper, and that those killers would be the same pair that had robbed his wife.

Keeping with their pattern of unpredictability, they next hit a liquor store that operated on the Missouri side of the bridge that connected two cities with the same name, Kansas City.

Venturing north along the Missouri River, on Saturday, September 28, they made an exception to their usual practice when they robbed a Hinky Dinky Supermarket in Omaha, Nebraska.

Like a pinball, they now ricocheted east, traveling the highways through the three adjacent "I" states: Iowa, Illinois, and just into Indiana.

On the evening of Sunday, September 29, 1957, they rested at a motel on US-20 on the outskirts of Gary, Indiana. Their full court press of the last week found them flush with cash. One can envision them toasting their continued success with more than two fingers of Old Taylor whiskey poured in a Dixie cup. Taylor undoubtedly had a name bias for this brand, keeping several bottles in the trunk of the Chevrolet.

With a toast complete, the drinking began, and with it the likely boasting of having committed more than 20 armed robberies in 14 states without detection. To Whitley, Taylor's ability to be invisible to the police had been proven. Until now, Whitley would have never guessed he could live so good so easily.

Sometime during their four-month rampage, the duo had added a second car to their fleet. They likely acquired the Plymouth station wagon, which was registered to Taylor, during one of their passes through Taylor's home state of West Virginia. Whether Taylor had purchased this car prior to or after going on the lam is not known.

As they drank, they counted their money. Once totaled, they decided that they now had enough cash on hand, along with the Plymouth as a trade, to purchase a new car. They thought, what better place to do it than Detroit, the Motor City.

Michigan was a state they had not yet done business in, adding assurance to their invisibility. But, before leaving Indiana, they would first go to area banks and change their small bills into big ones in preparation for the purchase.

It is likely that they schemed how they might use this transaction to put in play one of the sets of identification they had acquired in their travels. Identification that was tucked into a brown leather billfold, secluded in a black Samsonite bag, and stowed in the trunk of the car.

While they did not yet think the name Victor Whitley was on any wanted poster, Ralph Taylor's name might be, as he was pretty sure he was wanted for parole violation out of West Virginia.

Perhaps they planned for Taylor to change out his real identification for the credentials of Cecil R. Compeau of Uniontown, Pennsylvania. Taylor would then claim to be him when they brokered the vehicle transaction. Pretending to be Cecil Compeau, he would produce a title for the station wagon in the name of Ralph Taylor that was signed off and state that the owner, Ralph Taylor, had sold it to him.

Taylor would then be able to get the new car in the name of his alias, Cecil Compeau, providing him insulation from the warrant in his real name. This is but an example of one ruse they might have used; their exact plans remain unknown.

The author cannot resist taking a sidebar from the story to report the results of an internet query for the names Louis L. Schick and Cecil R. Compeau whose identification Taylor and Whitley had acquired. He discovered that men of those names and towns appear to have lived good full lives, which supports conjecture that Taylor and Whitley had acquired the credentials by theft.

Taylor and Whitley's plan would next take them into Michigan, a place neither had been before as mentioned previously. They studied the map for a route. They decided to go north into Michigan and then turn toward Detroit, traveling east on US-112 (present-day US-12).

PART B – Ten Hours

*"Other than random attacks, all such cases
begin with the decision of a police officer
to do something, to help, to arrest, to inquire.
If the officer had decided to do nothing,
then no force would have been used.
In this sense, the police officer always
causes the trouble. However, it is trouble which
the police officer is sworn to cause,
which society pays him to cause and which,
if kept within constitutional limits,
society praises the officer for causing."*
Plakas v. Drinski, 19 F.3d 1143 (7th Circuit 1994)

Chapter IV – MICHIGAN PRELUDE

In the darkness the patrol car idled, its headlights cast across the highway. Its beam provided the young troopers a glimpse of the occupants of passing vehicles as they motored either east or west on US-112. A trooper never knew what might be seen.

The shift had quieted as the day neared closure. Like the radio, Pellot's and Hutchinson's chatter had also silenced. In the calm, Pellot's mind wandered.

Pellot smiled to himself as he reminisced about the earlier day. It had been special. Kay, his wife, and he had even attended church. Working weekends had made church difficult, often impossible.

Pellot's thoughts then became more distant. The last time they had been to church had been in Lansing nearly a year ago when Greg, their now year-old son, was baptized. Lansing had always been their home until Pellot had graduated from the Michigan State Police Academy 16 months earlier. Graduation had been a turning point in his young family's life, more than he would ever know.

When graduation day finally arrived, they had anxiously awaited what would follow the emcee's introduction of "Trooper Dugald Allan Pellot." They knew the next words would be where he would be stationed. His name was followed with "Clinton Post." To them, Clinton was only a clue, as neither had ever heard of it.

During the congratulatory handshakes that followed the ceremony, the now Trooper Pellot asked an academy instructor where the Clinton Post was and heard "Look in the library." It appeared the hazing had not yet ended. He later learned that the post was actually in the Clinton Library.

Kay and Trooper Dugald Pellot on graduation day

Compliments of Kay Pellot Andersen

Pellot's thoughts returned to today. After church, it was home for a Sunday dinner and a bit of family time before reporting for duty. Then it was off to work the afternoon shift at the Clinton Post.

If he was honest, being on the road trooping was his most favorite place to be. There he patrolled with Trooper Warren Hutchinson. Hutch was a junior trooper to him, although just barely. Both were 23 years of age, both married with a baby, both living in nearby Tecumseh, and both having nearly identical Oldsmobile 98s. Pellot's was a yellow 1950, and Hutch's a green

1951. Their shared experiences on the road had bonded them as partners.

Pellot broke the silence. "Hutch, if anything happens to me out here, take care of my family."

"You know it, partner," Hutch answered. Moments passed. Hutch continued, "Ready to head in? It'll be quitting time by the time we get everything squared away."

Pellot's tone changed. "Yeah, I lost the flip. Got to double back and do fatigue tomorrow." Double back meant Pellot would have to return to duty eight hours after going off shift. Fatigue meant he would have to check each of the patrol cars assigned to the Clinton Post, making sure everything worked, contained the required equipment, and was clean inside and out.

Michigan troopers did not have take-home patrol cars. They drove their personal cars to work and then used patrol cars assigned to the post. Fatigue duty was a weekly ritual at all Michigan State Police posts. The good part of it was that afterward he could spend the evening at home with his young family.

"I bet my Olds can beat your Olds."

"We'll see on the way home."

And while Trooper Dug Pellot worked his Sunday afternoon shift, Kay, while Greg slept in his crib, caught up her diary for the past two days. She wrote:

Saturday 9/28/1957 –

. . . After Dug went to work I called Ilene Hutchinson and made arrangements for her to watch Greg on Sunday so Dug and I could go to church . . . and get something out of it. She was more than happy to do it.

I got Dug's church clothes out, made sure they were all in good order, then arranged them outside of the closet. I was in bed but awake when he got home. As usual the first thing he did when getting home from work was to go look at Greg in his crib, touch him gently, then come into the bedroom. I asked him if he would like to go to church in the morning. He looked at all his clothes by the closet, gave me that big "light up the world" smile of his and said, "Do I have a choice?" We had a good laugh about this.

Sunday 9/29/1957 –

Dropped Greg off at Ilene's, went to church. It was as though we were here, with all of these people, but I can only remember us, in our world ... a special day.

Picked up Greg, went home to have dinner as Dug had to go to work at 2:00 pm. We were all in the kitchen while I was fixing dinner. Dug played with Greg, tossing him up into the air, Greg would squeal like crazy we were all laughing having so much fun.

Times like this are precious because Dug is gone so much, working for the State of Michigan, they own him body and soul. I do hate this life, I'm jealous of his job, I want him all to myself. Maybe at 20 I'm too young to realize that this is life, grow up ... now! Greg and I are alone so much, we have no money. I had no idea that being a trooper's wife meant giving up life as most people know it. . .

The MSP was formed in 1917, but it would not be until 1933 that the agency implemented the blockade system. A blockade is where officers stop traffic at designated points leading away from the crime scene and check the vehicles for wanted suspects. Ironically, 1933 was also the year the Indiana State Police (ISP) was born. It seems that both blockades and the ISP were created, at least in part, to combat bank robberies.

Also, in the 1930s the iconic face of the Michigan State Police Post was built by the Civilian Conservation Corps (CCC). With few exceptions, they all had the same look, made of red brick and mortar. Based on current and projected population trends, they were placed strategically throughout the state. Citizens came to know them as a safe refuge, always open with a state police officer manning the desk.

In southern Michigan, many posts were built along US-112, the main thoroughfare between Detroit and Chicago. Among them were the Jonesville and Ypsilanti posts. In time, after the CCC had been disbanded, it was realized the 60 miles separating those two was a gap too far. Between the two was the Village of Clinton, and its citizens wanted a state police post so much that they volunteered space for it in their library. During the 1950s, the village library was the crowded beehive of troopers assigned to Clinton.

Since completing his field training and probationary period, Trooper Hutchinson mostly worked nights with Pellot, who had graduated from the recruit school before him. Both Pellot and Hutchinson were products of the "Hasty 200," a hiring initiative in 1956-57 to restore the depleted ranks of the MSP.

At just 27 years of age, Trooper Douglas Vogel's life had certainly been full. After graduating from high school and serving two years in the Navy, he returned home to marry Marilyn, his sweetheart of two years.

Shortly thereafter, he was accepted into the MSP. After recruit school, he was fortunate to be assigned to the Clinton Post, since it was only 20 miles from their hometown of Chelsea. They could have been stationed anywhere in the state.

With Vogel being assigned to Clinton, his dad, affectionately known as Bumpa by his grandkids, built his son's family a small, ranch-style house on the north side of Clinton. Here the young couple were raising four children with another on the way.

Vogel had excelled as a trooper. This had been acknowledged by his assignment as a field training officer, known as a senior officer during that era. Trooper Warren Hutchinson had been one of his cubs (probationary trooper), and they too had developed the bond of partners.

As a norm, Michigan troopers worked a week of afternoons, followed by a week of days, and then a week of midnights, ending their rotation with the coveted one weekend off a month. At that time, they patrolled alone during daylight hours and doubled up during hours of darkness. Vogel was now on his day shift rotation.

Vogel had a short drive to the Clinton Post. Squeezed into the library, the post had no space for a locker room. For that reason, Vogel wore his uniform to work, something that always garnered attention from the public. His route, first south then west, did not make him squint into the rising sun.

Having parked in the alley behind the post, he saw Pellot, wearing MSP coveralls over his civilian clothes. He was washing 426, one of the many patrol cars assigned to the Clinton Post and affectionately known as "Blue Gooses." With their patented blue paint, lone oscillating red light on the roof, and hood light that read, "State STOP Police," they were unique to the MSP. In 1957, the Blue Goose was either a Plymouth or a Dodge, powered by V-8 engines and having push-button shifters.

As Vogel walked to the back door, he likely called to Pellot by his nickname, saying, "Cochise, I'll take 426 when you're done washing it." Standing 6-02, weighing 187 pounds, with white-blond hair, piercing green eyes, and a quick smile, Pellot looked nothing like a Native American, his nickname born from contrast.

With that, Vogel went in the back door of the dual-purpose building. There he found Corporal Floyd Paruch manning the radio, and Sergeant Fred O'Donnell busy with post commander duties in their one and only office.

At age 45, O'Donnell was a twenty-year veteran. Since being promoted, he had been off the road, busy with supervision and administrative duties. Like most MSP post commanders, to his face, troopers called him "Sergeant," but behind his back, they referred to him as "The Old Man," in this case with respect.

The sergeant looked up from his paperwork to harass Vogel,

saying that he hoped he would shoot better at fall qualifications. O'Donnell was on the MSP pistol team and an expert shot. Going from outside to inside, the pecking order had changed. Vogel was now among superiors, and it was he they teased.

Vogel briefed himself for patrol by scanning the radio log, reading current materials, and meeting with Corporal Paruch. While Pellot finished up making sure patrol car 426 was ship-shape, Vogel, using both his index fingers, punched the keys of a manual typewriter, completing what seemed like never-ending paperwork.

Then, the back door swung open. Playfully, Pellot tossed the keys to 426 at Vogel as he said the Blue Goose was ready. Vogel looked up just in time to catch the keys before being hit by them. Good thing Pellot was off probation, or he would have been reprimanded for such abrupt behavior.

Before heading out, Vogel phoned his wife to see if her morning sickness had passed. She said she felt better. He wondered if it was true. A family, especially one his size, was a lot to support on a trooper's meager salary. But most troopers did not come from means, so they knew no different.

With briefcase in his left hand, shotgun in right, and garrison cap pressed on his head, Vogel exited the post. Bullet-resistant vests were still a thing of the future, something that would not come to the MSP until the mid-1970s. He strolled to his shiny Blue Goose to begin his day of patrol.

Whether left or right-handed, all Michigan troopers carried their revolver in a flapped cross-draw holster on their left hip. Being on the left hip gave them a uniform appearance, and, it could be argued, the gun could be drawn with either hand. It had become the holster of the MSP in 1927 after Corporal Sam Mapes was killed by a bootlegger who had come up behind him and had taken his revolver from his strong-side holster and then shot him in the back.

The flapped cross-draw holster was not fast draw, but it was secure. Most often, when a trooper was in contact with a potential threat, he had his hand in his right front pocket which held a concealed snub-nosed revolver. It was this gun a trooper could both quickly and unexpectedly brandish. "One for show and one for go," was how the MSP summed up their weapon system.

Vogel headed out on patrol to begin another day of hunting for that big arrest in the sky. Looking beyond the traffic offense was something he had been trained to do and something he passed on to those he trained. Troopers referred to it as "shaking cars."

It was Monday, September 30, 1957, and it had been born a glorious day in southern Michigan. Clear skies, with a hint of autumn crispness, did not lend warning of the approaching trouble.

Trooper Douglas Vogel

From FALLEN TROOPERS OF THE M.S.P. – V. BECK

> *"Hell is empty and all the devils are here."*
> ~ William Shakespeare ~

Chapter V – HOUR 1

As usual, things were going according to plan for Whitley and Taylor. After exchanging small bills for large ones at an Indiana bank, they crossed into Michigan, later turning east on US-112. They ate a late lunch at a diner in the vicinity of Coldwater, and then continued their trek toward Detroit with Whitley leading the duo in the Chevrolet.

Being near Detroit, the Irish Hills was a popular tourist area with its numerous lakes. Because of the many curves and hills in that stretch of US-112, the speed limit had been reduced. One can surmise that Whitley did not see the speed limit sign indicating the drop from 65 mph to 45 mph as they entered the Irish Hills. Taylor apparently did, and as always complied, not wanting to draw police attention. With a 20 mph speed difference, Whitley did not notice that he was pulling away from Taylor.

Afternoon found Trooper Vogel patrolling US-112 in the Irish Hills. Many citizens considered it a speed trap, and troopers allowed speeding motorists a 10 mph cushion before stopping them.

Whitley and Vogel first got a glimpse of each other's vehicles as they met in a curve. Seeing the patrol car, Whitley instinctively checked his speedometer – it showed 65 mph. Thinking, "No problem," he didn't slow down.

Vogel's Blue Goose was not equipped with a speed-detecting

device such as radar, but his experience told him the car was well over the cushion. Out of sight of the Chevrolet, Vogel mashed the brake as he steered to the shoulder. Nearly coming to a stop, he released the brake and pulled his front tires to the pavement where he now floored the accelerator. With the rear tires breaking traction and the front tires holding on the pavement, the Blue Goose spun around like a pinwheel. The maneuver was called a power turn and was the quickest way to change vehicular direction. He now sped after the Chevrolet until he caught sight of it. He then settled in, hoping to get a pace clock on the vehicle.

With the needle on the patrol car's speedometer holding at 60, the Chevy was pulling away. Vogel then sped up to 65 mph; now the Chevy only crept away. They then entered the curves that began just past Pentecost Highway. Vogel bided his time to make the traffic stop at the next straightaway as it would be safer there. As he did, he noticed that the Chevy had an out-of-state license plate.

If Whitley had been daydreaming, it ended when he spotted the reflection of the patrol car in his rearview mirror. He glanced down at his speedometer, the needle now nearing 70 mph. He eased up on the gas but did not touch the brakes, not yet. Again he glanced in his mirror; the Blue Goose seemed to be tailgating him.

Whitley probably asked himself, "Wasn't the speed limit 65? Surely, he wasn't going to stop him for just a couple of miles over." Whitley thought, "Remain calm."

Not wanting to appear to be rubbernecking, Whitley tried to nonchalantly look at his mirror for the third time. This time he looked beyond the patrol car, searching for Taylor's station wagon. It was nowhere to be seen. Whitley figured he was back there somewhere.

Whitley hoped the officer was on a call and looking to pass him, not stop him. But, if he did, he remembered their plan.

When they entered the straightaway by Evans Lake, near the motel sandwiched between the highway and the lake, Vogel accelerated alongside the Chevrolet, his red light on, and honked his horn. When the driver looked over, he pointed him to the side of the road. It was called the side-stop and was a common technique with the MSP until the 1970s.

Doing as they had planned, Whitley abruptly braked the Chevrolet and pulled to the shoulder. He braked so suddenly that Vogel was unable to pull in behind it. He settled for pulling the patrol car to the shoulder in front of the Chevrolet, not the preferred position. He would have to make do.

Eva Mann owned the Motel on Evans Lake where she also lived. Having just a few guests, she was enjoying a glorious autumn day lounging on her patio. Her attention was drawn from her lake view when she heard the powerful patrol car accelerate. She turned toward US-112 to see its red light flashing, on the far side of a green car with both cars headed east. The cars then disappeared from sight, blocked by her neighbor's cottage. Curious, she walked to the road to watch.

Right hand in his pocket, grasping the small snub-nosed revolver, Vogel walked back to the Chevrolet, noting that the driver and sole occupant was a clean-cut looking man of similar age to himself. He repeated his standard opening line, "Driver's license and registration, please."

Pleasantly the man said, "I don't have my license with me. The car belongs to my sister." Vogel could not know that the car was stolen and the man was a part of a multi-state armed robbery duo. The unidentified Whitley patronized the trooper, hoping he would buy his line and let him go. If he didn't, he wondered if Taylor would come to his rescue as planned.

As Vogel talked with the driver, he scanned the backseat of the Chevrolet for anything that didn't look right. He noticed a roll of wide white adhesive tape nested in cut lengths of rope. Not illegal, they still piqued his curiosity. With the driver unable to produce the required paperwork, Vogel had grounds to check further.

He had Whitley open the trunk. As Vogel began to go through

its contents, a blue 1953 Plymouth station wagon pulled in behind. The driver was a short, pudgy white male who looked to be in his thirties, a devil yet to be revealed. He walked up to Vogel, demanding to know what was going on.

Vogel's eyes met those of the intruder of his personal space and there was that momentary attempt to stare each other down. Neither blinked. Vogel barked back, "I'm running this show, go back to your car." A yet-to-be-identified Ralph Taylor lingered eye contact a moment longer before obeying, as if to silently say there would be a reckoning. He then walked back to his Plymouth. As he did, Vogel asked Whitley, "Is he with you?" Whitley said he was his uncle.

While Whitley acted passive, Taylor posed an intimidating demeanor. Vogel's instincts told him he was on to something; what it was, he wasn't sure. "Stay here," Vogel said to Whitley.

Taylor waited at the front of the Plymouth as Vogel walked back to him. As he did, Vogel noted that Taylor wore a cloth jacket that concealed his waistband. Vogel walked around him and peered through the open window into the backseat. His attention was drawn to a handkerchief suspiciously spread over a bag. He wondered what it might contain. Bending over, he reached into the backseat and pulled a cloth bag from beneath it. Bullets spilled onto the dusty shoulder of the roadway. And with that, all hell broke loose.

In Vogel's peripheral vision, he saw Taylor quickly approaching, his hand pointing a gun at Vogel's heart. With it now within arm's reach, Vogel's trooper training had taught him his best move was to grab the suspect's gun and twist it from his hand. He reached to do so. As he pushed the muzzle down, the pistol fired, its searing bullet striking Vogel in the abdomen.

"Oh my God," Vogel moaned as he fell to the ground and rolled into the ditch, his garrison cap tumbling from his head. By rolling down the incline he hoped to create distance while drawing his revolver. As he did, Taylor pursued him, shooting fast. Rolling against a willow tree, Vogel would now have to hold his ground.

Taylor's next heart shot just missed, the bullet burrowing into Vogel's chest just above it. As if directing traffic to stop, Vogel instinctively held up his left hand in defense while his right worked to remove his own gun from its flapped, cross-draw-holster. Designed to be secure, not necessarily fast, it was the quickest when two hands were used, the left to unsnap the flap that covered the weapon and the right to draw it.

The next shot struck Vogel's thumb, which spattered his face with blood. In that millisecond, Vogel again changed strategy. Having first applied the primal survival instinct of fight, followed by flight, he now transitioned to the less recognized one of freeze.

Sprawled in the ditch, his right hand resting on his holster's flap, Vogel played dead. There he listened to the metal mechanical sounds of the gun being cycled and wondered if it was true you don't hear the shot that kills you.

Had Taylor's gun jammed or had he emptied it on the now motionless trooper? Taylor, probably thinking he had surely killed the trooper with a heart shot and a head shot, ran back to his car.

Shot in the abdomen, upper chest, and thumb, Vogel switched back to the fight instinct as he heard the doors slam on the Plymouth and Chevrolet. Vogel was finally able to draw his gun as he struggled to his feet.

Revolver in hand, Vogel scrambled to the shoulder of the road. For accuracy reasons, he was trained to shoot single-action, where the hammer is manually cocked with the thumb, making for a lighter trigger pull. But now for speed he fired double-action, where the trigger both cocks and releases the hammer. Vogel quickly fired all six rounds of his revolver at the cars as they roared away. As Whitley led their flight east, swerving around the parked patrol car, one of Vogel's bullets struck his Chevy.

Vogel stumbled to his Blue Goose. Once seated, he keyed the microphone with his mangled thumb and gasped, "I've been shot."

The attentive desk officer at the Clinton Post, Corporal Floyd

Paruch, heard the three forlorn words. He noted the time as 3:05 p.m., which he would later type on the radio log. That time would come to mark the kick off of ten hours of terror that would span two states.

The corporal had recognized Vogel's voice and its tone. His years of experience had taught him that tone could communicate nearly as much as words. He tried to radio him back to learn more but couldn't. In the shock of Vogel's injuries, he had not released the push-to-talk button on the microphone, preventing the post from being able to answer.

Corporal Paruch knew from Vogel's previous radio traffic that he had been patrolling US-112 near Evans Lake. It just so happened that Trooper Frank Francisco was in the post as Trooper Clair Dechow stopped in. The corporal directed them to double up and head that way in hopes of finding Vogel.

As they sprinted to their patrol car, they passed Pellot washing another and said, "Vogel's been shot." Pellot could not have heard Vogel's radio traffic because at that time, one patrol car could not hear another patrol car's radio traffic. It had to be relayed by the post.

Pellot ran into the post where Sergeant O'Donnell was grabbing a shotgun from the gun locker. He handed it to Pellot, saying, "Come with me." While all the shotguns at the post were Winchesters, Pellot recognized this one as his least favorite. There was no time to exchange it for another. With the sergeant taking the driver's seat, Pellot jumped in. Only minutes behind Troopers Francisco and Dechow, they too raced west on US-112.

From where Eva Mann watched, she became a witness to the fast-paced nightmare. With the Chevrolet and Plymouth fleeing east, she hurried to check on the trooper. She found Vogel slumped in the patrol car, badly wounded, but still conscious.

It was about then that Vogel realized that his injured thumb had not answered his brain's order to release the button on the microphone. He switched hands, clearing the air so that the post could now radio him.

Prompted by the corporal, Vogel radioed, "I've been shot by an older man, short in height and wearing a cloth jacket. Believed armed with a semi-automatic pistol. He fled east in a blue Plymouth station wagon with an out-of-state license plate. He is traveling with a man younger than him who has a light complexion and is wearing khaki clothing. The second man is driving a '54 Chevrolet coupe which also has out-of-state license plates."

A neighbor brought Eva Mann a towel, and with it, she tried to slow the profuse bleeding of his thumb. Vogel's bleeding abdomen and chest wound were mostly concealed by his shirt. As she helped, Vogel told her to retrieve his cap from the ditch. When she returned with it, he had her light him a cigarette. He inhaled deeply its soothing smoke as he anxiously waited for the troopers and ambulance to arrive.

As Whitley led Taylor east on US-112, he was careful not to speed as he did not want to draw attention. He wished he had not been careless earlier. His mind raced with what had just occurred. Taylor had said he would never be taken alive, and he was always talking of tactics on how to get away. One of Taylor's contingency plans, having Whitley lead in the stolen car so that if the police stopped him, Taylor could intercede, had just played out.

Then a blue patrol car rounded the curve, racing west, its red light and siren ablaze. After they met, Whitley watched in his mirror for it to brake, but it did not. Unless the trooper had bled out, he knew it was just a matter of time before the police would have their vehicle descriptions and last seen direction of travel. According to their plans, it was time to change course and look for a new car. Whitley decided to turn south at the next paved road.

Moments later, the corporal broadcast Vogel's description of his assailants and their vehicles. The patrol car Whitley and Taylor had just met contained Troopers Dechow and Francisco. Minutes later these troopers located Vogel and cared for him until the ambulance from Proctors Funeral Home in Clinton arrived.

Back then, funeral homes were dual purpose: hearse and ambulance. When the ambulance arrived, it transported Vogel, with Trooper Francisco at his side, the 33 miles to St. Joseph Hospital in Ann Arbor. Trooper Dechow remained at the scene.

The next paved road was North Adrian Highway, and Whitley followed another car turning south with Taylor tailgating him in the station wagon. Glancing left, Whitley saw another blue patrol car going west on US-112. This one turned, following them.

In his mirror, Whitley saw the patrol car fall in behind Taylor's station wagon, red light flashing. When he looked forward, the car in front of him pulled to the shoulder. Whitley, Taylor, and the patrol car passed the car. Whitley could no longer resist speeding up, but Taylor did not.

The passed car, having yielded to the patrol car with the flashing light, now followed the entourage. Like Eva Mann of Evans Lake, Bernie Hague of Onsted was about to become a witness to a real-life nightmare.

As he drove, Sergeant O'Donnell radioed the post, "We are following two vehicles matching the description south on North Adrian Highway. One is a Plymouth station wagon bearing West Virginia license plate 425 086. The other is a green-and-white Chevrolet with outstate license plate with the letters SD, unable to see the numbers."

While the Chevrolet sped away, the Plymouth maintained a speed of 45 mph, its driver acting oblivious to the trailing patrol car. Calling Pellot by his abbreviated first name, the sergeant said to him, "Dug, when I pull alongside the car, if he doesn't stop, shoot out a tire."

Pellot rolled down his window. Confined to the passenger seat of the patrol car, he racked a round into the chamber of the shotgun and then awkwardly turned to his right, aiming the muzzle out the window.

As Whitley watched in his mirror, he wondered if Taylor would do as they had planned. He saw the patrol car pull alongside his partner, a barrel pointed out its window. Then, just like Taylor had taught, the station wagon braked abruptly and pulled to the shoulder. Whitley crested the hill and the drama disappeared from his mirror.

With an action being faster than a reaction, the patrol car was unable to stop as fast, coming to a halt a bit ahead of the Plymouth.

Taylor had not had time to reload the Savage pistol he had shot Trooper Vogel with, but he had other guns. He grasped the Smith & Wesson, holding it out of sight. Staying with his rules of engagement, Taylor had picked the spot to do battle and knew that the first accurate shot won. He now needed to draw the officer in close to make an easy heart shot.

Like Whitley's maneuver earlier, Taylor's ploy had tactically compromised the position of the officers. They would have to go with it, the sergeant yelling to Pellot, "Watch that fellow close, Dug, and I'll get the other one." Having to deal with being positioned badly, Pellot sprang from the patrol car, shotgun aimed at the Plymouth's driver.

Taylor may have been surprised to see a young Aryan-looking man, clad in coveralls and carrying a shotgun, emerge from the patrol car. As Pellot cautiously approached, shotgun at the ready, the driver of the Plymouth leaned his head out the window and nonchalantly said, "Sorry about your car door."

When Pellot glanced at the patrol car, Taylor quickly made a heart shot. The large-caliber bullet was deflected upward when it struck the barrel of the shotgun leveled at him. Instead of hitting the heart, the bullet severed Pellot's aorta artery, causing a catastrophic loss of blood pressure and near-instant unconsciousness.

The sergeant was just pulling away when he heard the shot. He turned to see Pellot collapsing, the shotgun dropping from his hands. Again he stopped the patrol car, this time exiting the driver's door and slipping. As he fell, Taylor's next shot passed through space O'Donnell had just filled.

Using the patrol car for cover, the sergeant crept to the trunk from where he returned fire, putting a round through the windshield and rear-view mirror of the station wagon.

Plymouth station wagon that Sergeant O'Donnell fired upon

From FALLEN TROOPERS OF THE M.S.P. – V. BECK

The Plymouth lurched forward as its driver again shot at the sergeant. As the Plymouth fled, the sergeant fired on it three more times. In the exchange, one of the bullets grazed the driver's head.

Never before, but twice today, Taylor's plan had worked: Do the unexpected by picking the spot, get them close, distract them, shoot them in the heart. Taylor's station wagon roared away.

The sergeant ran to his fallen trooper. The wound looked fatal. As he cared for Pellot, Bernie Hague, who had been driving the car the entourage had just passed and who had then witnessed the shootout, came to his side offering help.

"Do you have a blanket?" the sergeant asked. The man nodded. "Go get it and take care of Dug while I get the man who did this."

Back in the patrol car, the sergeant radioed for an ambulance as he sped south in hopes of overtaking the station wagon. Cresting the next hill, he saw nothing. He decided to return to Pellot and do what he could until the ambulance arrived. Again kneeling at the side of the fallen trooper, Sergeant O'Donnell did not want what he saw to be true. Pellot looked dead.

Please excuse an author sidebar. In 1976, on my first night of patrol as a probationary trooper, I recall a question my field training officer posed to me. If I was shot and appeared dead, did I want him to stay with me or go get the person who had shot me? My answer was revenge. Looking back, it would appear to be a tenet that had been handed down through generations of troopers.

Whitley drove until he got to the stop sign for M-50. Dutifully, he waited on the side of the road for what might come, be it the police or Taylor. He knew that within a minute or two he would know. If the police appeared, he would give up as he had no gun. His Mauser was stowed in the Plymouth.

If it was Taylor, they would continue as a team. Remembering their contingency plans, he bet Taylor would now have them double back and then look to commandeer a new getaway car.

Then, in his mirror he saw the station wagon approaching. With no time to talk, Taylor passed him and turned west on M-50. Whitley followed.

As the sergeant knelt by Pellot, waiting for the ambulance, he noticed a car approaching from the south. It appeared to be the station wagon with which he had just exchanged gunfire.

Preparing for the worst, the sergeant grabbed from the ground the shotgun Pellot had carried, racking it to make sure it was ready for service. When he did, a live round was ejected, the round Pellot had not had time to fire. While the gathering spectators scattered to the ditches for cover, the sergeant marched to the center of the road to confront the car, pointing the shotgun menacingly.

As the station wagon got closer, he could see that it was neither the same car nor the same man. It was what was commonly referred to as a look-alike. He lowered the shotgun. This car was driven by a minister returning home from Tecumseh. The sergeant asked if he had seen the Chevrolet or Plymouth. The minister had not.

The attendants from Collins Funeral Home in Tecumseh quickly loaded the fallen trooper into their ambulance and rushed him the four miles to nearby Herrick Hospital as they hoped for a miracle. It was the same hospital where Pellot had once witnessed a miracle, the birth of his son. And it would be Herrick Hospital where Coroner Braun would pronounce Trooper Dugald Pellot dead upon arrival. From his chest, near his heart, a .44 caliber bullet was removed. It would later be matched to Taylor's Smith & Wesson revolver.

Corporal Paruch, the desk officer, was busy, very busy. Never before, but now twice in ten minutes, he had summoned ambulances for shot troopers. His next priority was activating the blockade system. And as if doing two things at once, he also began calling in off-duty troopers to help hunt for the killers.

Hutchinson, scheduled to start work at 4:00 p.m., was in uniform and just getting ready to leave for the Clinton Post when his wife answered the phone. She yelled to him, "Dug's been shot. They need you at the post."

As Hutchinson now raced his Oldsmobile back to the post, his mind flashed to what Pellot had said to him the night before: "Hutch, if anything happens to me out here, take care of my family." At the post, he and Trooper Dechow, who had been relieved at the scene of Vogel's shooting, doubled up in one patrol car. They were assigned to freelance for the wanted duo west of the incidents.

Although not first on the priority list, notifying Vogel's and Pellot's wives needed to be completed as soon as possible. Policy

44

required it to be done by a superior officer.

Whitley followed Taylor west on M-50. He knew if things went as they had previously discussed, Taylor would be looking to change cars. As they neared the burg of Springville, Taylor braked for a blue Studebaker in front of him, which then made a right turn onto Bryan Highway. As it did, he could see it was driven by an old man. Taylor turned with it and Whitley followed, his breath quickening as he anticipated Taylor's next move.

At age 72, Harry Crowe was still spry. A World War I veteran, he was employed at two jobs: factory worker and farmer. He was returning home from his day job in Tecumseh to work his farm when in his mirror he noticed two cars tailgating him. They stuck right behind him as he turned right on Bryan Highway and kept close when he went left on Jessup Road. As he neared home, the Plymouth station wagon suddenly roared around him and forced him off the road. Sensing trouble, Crowe looked in his mirror to see the Chevrolet had him blocked from the rear.

When Crowe again looked forward, the driver of the Plymouth stood at his door, pearl-handled gun in his hand. Taylor was now implementing another part of their plan, impersonating the police. He said, "Do you realize you had been exceeding the speed limit?" Crowe argued he had not as Whitley joined them.

With his partner now at his side, Taylor then changed his role by abruptly saying, "Get out, we need a getaway car. We've killed two cops today, and if there is any trouble from you, I will put one right in the middle of your forehead."

They hustled Crowe back to the Chevrolet where the rope and white adhesive tape, that had earlier piqued Trooper Vogel's attention waited for use. Just as in their armed robberies, Whitley bound their victim: first hands, then feet, and then gagged him.

Taylor took Crowe's billfold and stole from it all his cash, a $10 bill and two $5 bills, stuffing them into his own billfold. Whitley then pushed Crowe into the back seat of the Chevrolet and pressed him onto its floorboard, menacingly telling him not to get out for an hour.

The duo now hurriedly moved their personal property from the Plymouth and Chevrolet to the Studebaker. During this transfer, Whitley armed himself with the Mauser, which he took from the Plymouth. While they would leave behind many of their personal items, they made sure to take the black Samsonite bag containing the documents they planned to use to one day assume new identities.

From the floorboard, Crowe then heard what he thought was the Plymouth being driven into the adjacent corn field that was awaiting harvest. Not long afterwards was the sound of car doors slamming, and then he recognized the noise of his Studebaker's engine fading into the distance.

Crowe realized they had stolen his car, leaving in exchange the Plymouth and Chevrolet. After just a few minutes of stillness, Crowe wriggled to free himself.

Chapter VI – HOUR 2

Whitley drove Taylor northwest toward Jackson in their freshly carjacked Studebaker, careful not to speed. As he did, he met a blue patrol car, the fourth since three o'clock, along with a white one, both racing south with lights flashing. Having just switched cars, the felons were once again invisible.

While Whitley wheeled the vehicle, Taylor excitedly reloaded the Savage and the Smith & Wesson, the guns with which he had just shot two troopers. As he reloaded the Smith & Wesson revolver, he unknowingly dropped a spent cartridge on the floorboard. During this time, Taylor bragged about the second police shootout and how he had distracted the young trooper with the ruse of the damaged car door, enabling him to make the kill with a heart shot.

Crowe, having been left bound in the backseat of the Chevrolet, did not wait the hour as ordered. He estimated later it took him about twenty minutes to free himself. When he emerged from the Chevrolet, he saw the telltale tire tracks into the field of tall corn. He figured the tracks would end at the station wagon. His Studebaker was gone.

He then walked as fast as a recently bound old man could to the nearest house, which was closer than his home. It was just after 4:00 p.m. when he telephoned Edward Kamke, the nearby Onsted constable, and told him what had happened. In Crowe's excitement, he overlooked telling him they had taken his Studebaker. The constable said he would be right over.

Once there, the constable learned of the Studebaker being stolen. He then relayed that information to the Clinton Post, along with his other findings, including that the abandoned Chevrolet and Plymouth had bullet holes in them.

Having told the constable to preserve the vehicles for fingerprints and any other evidence they might contain, the MSP desk officer broadcast an update. The murderers were now believed to be in a blue 1952 Studebaker displaying Michigan license plate UR-1973.

In that Pellot was dead and Vogel seriously wounded, Marilyn Vogel became first in the line of notifications. She likely gasped when she opened the door of her home to recognize Sergeant Fred O'Donnell and Detective Sergeant Leslie Wykes.

In short order, they told her that her husband had been hurt and was at St. Joseph Hospital being treated and that the detective would drive her there. She quickly arranged for the care of her four children, and they departed at 4:07 p.m.

Living close to Collins Funeral Home in Tecumseh, Trooper Pellot's wife, Kay, had heard the ambulance's siren that afternoon, not that unusual. It would not be until 4:20 p.m. that she would realize "For Whom the Bell Tolls."

Her first clue would be when Jean, the wife of Trooper Ray Valley, appeared at her back door. Ray and her husband had attended the same academy class, and both had been assigned to the Clinton Post. Through that process, Kay and Jean had become the best of friends.

As Kay walked to Jean, she sensed stress. As their eyes met, a knock came from the front door. Kay turned, and through the window, she could see uniforms. It was Corporal Floyd Paruch and Trooper Ray Valley.

While she hadn't, Kay's initial concern was that Jean had come to warn her that she was in trouble for something she had not even done, gossiping official state police business.

Kay would soon realize that Jean was there to support her when the officers told her that her husband had been killed. Holding their son Greg, she slumped on the couch, saying, "Notify Dug's mom in Lansing." A moment of silence reigned. She then turned to Jean and said, "Tell me it's not true."

As the new reality set in, reporters from the Detroit Free Press barged into Kay's living room. A light bulb flashed twice as reporters took two pictures of a newly distraught widow holding all she had left. The picture would appear in the newspaper's next edition and later in a magazine. The surprised troopers quickly ordered the reporters from the home and then posted a guard to prevent it from happening again.

Kay and Greg Pellot

Picture from TRUE DETECTIVE – Jan 1958

With the intrusion gone, Kay's eyes met those of Trooper Ray Valley, with whom Dug had attended trooper training. And, as if a time-out from her shock, she said to him, "Do you remember the night I sneaked pizza into the academy Quonset hut where you guys bunked?" With tears streaming down his cheeks, Ray nodded. Now looking at Greg, whom she cradled in her arms, she said, "I was five months pregnant with him when I did that."

Twenty miles later, Whitley found himself driving through the city of Jackson. The slower traffic would make for a good place to troll for another getaway car. "Follow that red-and-white Buick," is something Taylor would have likely said. Not only was the car flashy, but so was the red-headed woman who drove it.

Dorothea LeCronier worked full-time as a bank clerk and part-time as a drama teacher. It was not unusual for drama teachers to carry costumes, wigs, and the like in their cars. Donna, as she preferred to be called, was on her way home from her day job when she stopped at an A&P store to buy groceries. As she left, she glanced at the store clock; it read 4:20 p.m. She would have to hurry if she was going to have dinner ready for her schoolteacher husband at their usual time.

As LeCronier drove to her Jackson home, she turned south on Blackstone Street from Washington Street. It was near there that her attention was first drawn to a blue car when it pulled alongside her. She looked over to see two men in it, the passenger motioning her to pull over. She paid it no mind; it wasn't the first time she had drawn male attention.

Three turns later, now on Union Street in a more residential area, the same car started to pass and then forced her to the curb. A pudgy man stepped from its passenger door and quickly walked to her passenger door saying, "I'm a federal agent and you ran that stop sign. Show me your driver's license."

"No, I didn't. Show me your badge," the feisty LeCronier demanded.

With that, Taylor quickly opened the door and slid into the seat beside her, pulling his Smith & Wesson revolver from a shoulder holster. Pointing it from his lap, he ordered, "Follow the blue car."

Seeing Taylor's nod, Whitley led them west on Union Street and then north on Wisner Street where he stopped. Taylor yelled to him, "Find a more secluded spot; we'll follow you."

Whitley drove on, selecting a spot at the Jackson city limits, not far from the intersection of Washington and Brown Streets. Here Taylor took LeCronier from her Buick and shoved her into the backseat of the Studebaker. There waited the precut rope and adhesive tape they had earlier transferred from the Chevrolet.

Whitley knew what to do: bind and gag the woman while Taylor kept a lookout. Whitley wrapped and knotted the clothesline around LeCronier's hands, and then feet. While he did, Taylor rambled on to the attractive woman, repeatedly saying, "I'm sorry I shot the officer, but I had to do it for what Bob had done. If Bob had turned right, I wouldn't had to shoot the officer."

For a second one might think that Taylor was expressing a bit of remorse, but his words lack credibility when you recognize he was not referring to Whitley by his real name.

As if wanting to impress the woman, Taylor opened his jacket to expose a semi-automatic pistol on each hip. LeCronier probably didn't recognize them as a .32 Colt and a .380 Savage. The shoulder holster hung empty as Taylor held the Smith & Wesson .44 revolver, the one he had used to kill Trooper Pellot. It was with the .380 that he had shot Trooper Vogel.

Realizing that Whitley had no gag, Taylor pulled his crusty handkerchief from his pants pocket. Sensing what was going to happen, LeCronier pleaded, "No! Please use the one in my purse."

In the few minutes they had been together, Taylor apparently had developed a fondness for the spirited woman. He obliged her request by having Whitley bring her purse to the Studebaker. As he rifled through it looking for her handkerchief, LeCronier said, "If you're looking for money, I have little. I spent all but a dollar or two for groceries." Taylor found her handkerchief and used it to gag her.

Taylor doted on LeCronier by saying, "You're in tough shape then, but you have been good about the whole thing." Taylor pulled his billfold from his pocket and opened it for her to see several $100 bills, saying, "We've got plenty of money. I'll leave you this." He then removed two $5 bills and one $10 bill and laid them on her purse. It was the money Taylor had stolen from Crowe earlier.

While Taylor attempted to impress LeCronier, Whitley transferred their personal belongings between vehicles, this time from the Studebaker to the Buick. Once again, he made sure the Samsonite bag whose contents were important to their future plans wasn't left behind. As he did, he came across a map of Michigan. Quickly he studied it, memorizing a route to Indiana: take M-60 southwest from Jackson, and then M-66 south through Sturgis, which would then take them into Indiana.

True to form, they stuffed the now bound and gagged LeCronier onto the rear floorboard of the car. As they did, Taylor continued to talk to her saying, "I had a redhead back home. Spent three grand on her, even bought her a mink coat. One time, she held the gun for me."

Taylor glanced at his watch, and his words returned to the business at hand. "It's 4:26 p.m. Stay down for an hour and you won't be hurt." The door slammed, and as they walked away, LeCronier plainly heard one of them say, "We'll head for Albion." Then, more like a whisper, she heard, "We better head for the border fast." Moments later she heard her Buick motor away.

By 4:40 p.m. all the pre-planned blockade points were filled. At each blockade, one officer stood near the centerline of the road where he stopped all cars. He made contact with the driver and looked in each car to make sure the wanted men were not inside. On the side of the road was the second officer, using a patrol car for cover. Usually armed with a 12-gauge shotgun, this officer kept a sharp eye for a blue Studebaker and carefully monitored his partner's contacts, ready to fire if necessary. And with each contact, most citizens asked the same question, "What's going on?"

At these blockade points, with resolve in their eyes, troopers, deputies, and officers stood in harm's way. No matter their title, each hoped they would be the one that would bring justice to the deadly duo. The net had been cast.

Michigan Blockade Point

Picture from OFFICIAL DETECTIVE STORIES - Jan 1958

At 4:51 p.m. just as hour two was ending, news came from the doctors at St. Joseph Hospital in Ann Arbor. It appeared that the badly wounded Trooper Doug Vogel was going to survive.

Chapter VII – HOUR 3

Donna LeCronier squirmed to free herself as she fended off claustrophobia. Since she was bound, ten minutes probably felt like an hour. Finally, she was able to get herself onto the seat and sit up. In that position, her odd appearance drew the attention of Claud Hubbard, a passing motorist.

Not sure what he had just seen, Hubbard drove back by to take a second look. Seeing a gagged woman peering out the back window of a Studebaker concerned him. It was 5:10 p.m. when he called the Jackson City Police.

The Jackson Police responded quickly. At 5:20 p.m. they reported to the state police that the Studebaker had been found and that the duo was now believed to be in a red-and-white 1955 Buick with Michigan license plate KJ 2634. The state police hurried to relay the new information to all the blockade points and then to the public radio stations.

Charlie Southworth, an MSP Detective Sergeant assigned out of Fourth District Headquarters, had earlier been dispatched to Lenawee County to assist with the chaos that had erupted. Traveling southeast on M-50 in an unmarked detective car, he took up an observation point at the south end of the Village of Brooklyn where M-124 intersected M-50. There he first watched for the Chevrolet and Plymouth that Whitley and Taylor had last been seen in. During this time period it is likely that Whitley, driving Taylor northwest on M-50 in the Studebaker, passed him by.

When he later received the updated broadcast, he began watching for the Studebaker. Shortly after 5:20 p.m., Southworth received another updated broadcast. The duo was now thought to be in a red-and-white Buick. Immediately following the broadcast, he was dispatched back to Jackson. Once there, he was to interview Donna LeCronier, process the now recovered Studebaker for evidence, and canvass the area for witnesses.

Police interview of Dorothea LeCronier

Picture from TRUE DETECTIVE – Jan 1958

In Southworth's witness search he located an 8-year-old girl named Joanie Worden. She lived near where the desperadoes exchanged the Studebaker for the Buick. She was playing in her yard when she noticed the way the two men kept looking around as they moved things from one car to another. She did not see a woman. Before her mom called her to dinner, she saw them drive away in the red-and-white car. When Southworth asked which way they went, she pointed. Southworth noted that it was west on Michigan Avenue. Young Joanie described the men and said she would recognize them if she ever saw them again.

As Whitley drove them west from Jackson, Taylor studied the map. He agreed with Whitley's proposed route to Indiana, instincts telling him the sooner they left Michigan the better. Thinking back to his prison days, he couldn't remember the name of the fellow convict who had told him of the double-back tactic, but today, so far, it had served them well.

One can bet they had the Buick's radio turned on, listening for information about their rampage. They were likely relieved each time they heard the description of the Studebaker. The broadcast included the phone number of the state police.

As command of the manhunt shifted to MSP Fourth District Headquarters in Jackson, so did the flood of phone calls about possible sightings. It was an all-hands-on-deck situation and Sergeant Horvath found it necessary for him also to be answering the phone. They hoped for a tip that would lead to the duo.

At 5:25 p.m., the information on the Buick was sent over police frequencies, to be followed by the public radio broadcast. During that same minute, he again answered a ringing phone, "State Police, Sergeant Horvath."

A man's voice blurted, "I'm one of the guys you're looking for, but I didn't do the killing. I want to give myself up. Can't talk anymore; my partner is coming back. We're headed for Albion." The line went dead.

Horvath cradled the receiver. As he dictated the information to the typist keeping the log, he pondered the call. He knew there were less than 30 miles between Jackson and Albion and that nearly an hour had passed since the duo left the woman bound in the Studebaker. If true, this phone call presented a break that might allow police to catch up to the elusive pair. Regardless, the information could not be ignored.

Later analysis would suggest that as Whitley and Taylor neared Sturgis, they stopped to change drivers. When they did, one of them made the phone call. The author was unable to determine which of the two did. A little more than a half hour had passed when Taylor then drove Whitley across the line into Indiana. Albion had been a ruse.

Many police blockades were placed on M-60. But apparently the duo wiggled through in the Buick while officers still watched for the Studebaker, or else they were set up behind them.

Their time in Michigan had been short but intense. It had not gone entirely as planned, but in many ways it had. So far, their contingency plans had kept them free.

With their exodus from Michigan, they hoped to become even more invisible. It was just after 6:00 p.m. and hunger pangs were beginning to haunt them.

Chapter VIII – HOURS 4 - 5

From all over the state's lower peninsula, troopers were sent to southern Michigan to bolster the manhunt. With the pre-planned blockade points already filled, command now looked to expand the road blocks to include as many secondary roads as possible. There was no way to know if the duo had gotten by the trap before it was set or if they were holed up somewhere.

The command center, having begun in the combination post and library in Clinton, had then transitioned to Fourth District Headquarters in Jackson. By early evening, command was at departmental headquarters in East Lansing, where the commissioner of the Michigan State Police, Joseph A. Childs, took charge. He too wondered who the demons might be.

In the operations room, a large plotting map of southern Michigan covered one wall. On it, staff tracked patrol car positions and the many possible sightings. Soon into the hunt, Commissioner Childs realized they might have failed to contain the threat. He had the authorities in the border states, Ohio and Indiana, warned.

And while officers searched for the killers, investigators examined four crime scenes for clues that might reveal more information about the criminals they sought and where they might go or hide.

Detectives scoured the first crime scene where Vogel's intuition had sparked a firestorm. It was a place where, for just a few minutes in time, patrol car 426, a Chevrolet, and a Plymouth paths crossed on the shoulder of the highway.

Easily found on its dusty shoulder were live .44 caliber rounds, some still in the bag Vogel had dropped from the station wagon. Being randomly scattered made it more difficult to find the spent

.380 cartridges, ejected from the Savage semi-automatic pistol as it fired three bullets into the trooper.

Like the first crime scene, the second one, where Pellot had been slain, had nearly evaporated. While Sergeant O'Donnell helped the detectives reconstruct the scene, he spotted a live round of 12-gauge buckshot on the edge of the road. His curiosity was quelled when he realized it was the round he had ejected from the shotgun Pellot had carried, as the look-alike station wagon had approached the scene.

Two ironies waited to be recognized. Where Taylor had chosen to do his second battle, killing Trooper Pellot, was at the intersection of Taylor Road. The other was that Trooper Douglas Vogel and Ralph Taylor had the same birthday.

In comparison, the third scene had the potential to produce an abundance of information. It was on Jessup Road where Harry Crowe had been carjacked of his Studebaker. Here the abandoned Chevrolet and Plymouth awaited processing.

Since the Chevrolet displayed a South Carolina license plate, a call was placed to the South Carolina Highway Patrol requesting registration information. At 6:45 p.m., the South Carolina Highway Patrol phoned back and reported that license plate, SD 128, had been reported lost or stolen from a 1949 Ford some 7 to 10 days earlier. Because of a discrepancy in the serial number of the Chevrolet, it would not be until 3:00 p.m. the next day that it was learned that the vehicle had been stolen on May 7, 1957, in Portsmouth, Ohio.

A similar phone call was made to the West Virginia State Police. At 7:00 p.m., they called back and reported that West Virginia license plate 452 086 belonged on a 1953 Plymouth station wagon registered to Ralph Taylor in St. Albans, West Virginia. With that information, Michigan asked West Virginia to look into Ralph Taylor as a person of interest in the murder of a Michigan trooper. Trooper Eddy of the West Virginia State Police said, "I'll get right on it and call you back with what I find."

At 9:32 p.m., West Virginia State Police called back with their findings. Ralph Walter Taylor, age 35, FBI number 5018052, was described as being 5-06 and 175 pounds with medium brown hair and blue eyes. Checks on the name revealed that he had served time for rape, was currently wanted for a parole violation, and was considered armed and dangerous. Contact with his parole officer indicated that Taylor had been detained by the Navarre, Ohio, police on May 31, 1957, but had somehow gotten free before extradition could be arranged.

The description of Taylor matched that of the man who had shot Vogel and Pellot. Arrangements were made for a picture of Taylor to be sent to Michigan the fastest way – airmail. For the time being, the MSP now had a name that might belong to one of the two suspects. The picture would arrive too late.

Prison picture of Ralph Taylor

From FALLEN TROOPERS OF THE M.S.P. – V. BECK

Pursuing this information further, the West Virginia State Police (WVSP) came up with two addresses for Taylor; one was his dad's and the other was his sister's. Having provided the information requested, WVSP then volunteered to stake out both addresses. Contact was also made with the local police where Ralph Taylor was from. They described him as having a split personality, good and evil.

Constable Kamke and a trooper waited with the two abandoned cars while crime scene technicians responded from East Lansing headquarters. With darkness approaching, these officers searched the grounds surrounding the two vehicles for anything of evidentiary value.

Found in the roadway was a man's watch, wrapped in tissue paper held by a rubber band. Scattered on the ground near the Plymouth were receipts from Biloxi, Mississippi, and Ashland, Kentucky.

It was dark when the crime technicians arrived. Constable Kamke, who also owned and operated a repair shop, volunteered to have the cars towed to his garage in Onsted where they could be processed in the light.

Once the cars were towed there, the technicians dusted key locations of the vehicles and certain items for latent fingerprints. Fingerprints were lifted from mirrors, windows, steering wheels, and liquor containers, one being a bottle of Old Taylor whiskey.

With a bullet hole in the trunk of the Chevrolet, technicians searched for the projectile responsible for it. Inside the trunk they found a .38 caliber bullet, likely fired from Vogel's revolver.

On the front floorboard of the Plymouth station wagon, they found two .38 caliber bullets. They were later determined to have been fired from Sergeant O'Donnell's Colt revolver when he exchanged shots with its driver.

Also found between the two cars were a variety of items that the duo had left behind when they hurriedly changed from the two cars to the Studebaker. These items, when considered, revealed information about the suspects.

In the two cars, the following noteworthy items were found:
- License plates from Missouri, Massachusetts, and Kentucky.
- Money bags from Mallon National Bank & Trust and from
  Hancock County National Bank in Garner, Iowa.
- Motel receipts from various states.
- Pry bars and blackjacks, a type of bludgeon weapon.
- A name and address in Myrtle Beach, South Carolina.

The fourth crime scene was the recovered stolen Studebaker in which Donna LeCronier had been found bound and gagged. From it Detective Sergeant Southworth lifted six latent fingerprints.

Taken as evidence were the rope and gag used to restrain her. Additionally, a small, brown, zippered shaving kit bag was found which contained two 4-foot lengths of rope, two rolls of 1-inch-wide adhesive tape, and a gag made of tissue. Such findings suggested, at the least, that the police had encountered organized criminals. Also in the shaving kit was an envelope with the address 314 S. Spring St. Cape Girardeau, Missouri. The envelope held $5 in dimes, $5 in nickels, and also a roll of nickels. It likely originated from the finance company they had robbed there. Elsewhere in the Studebaker was what was believed to be the suspects' shirts, shoes, and underclothing.

Missed in the initial search of the Studebaker was the spent .44 caliber casing that Taylor had dropped while reloading. When later discovered, this casing would be matched to the Smith & Wesson .44 caliber revolver that Taylor carried, which would be matched to the bullet that killed Pellot.

On paper, this may appear as a calm, coordinated response. Do not be fooled. With 400 or more officers responding, there was undoubtedly immense chaos and confusion. The radio system would have been quickly overwhelmed. One of the MSP's aircraft was also sent, but its radio was defective, making it unable to transmit.

While officers manned blockade points, others stopped and responded to reports of sightings of a red-and-white Buick and men who fit the descriptions of the two suspects. Like Sergeant O'Donnell's earlier sighting of the station wagon which he thought contained the killer of Trooper Pellot, experienced officers come to know that when you watch for something specific, you often spot many who look alike. At the risk of offending innocent citizens, an officer must guard against dismissing sightings by a look-alike assumption, as it could make for a fatal mistake.

As time wore on, appreciative citizens brought coffee and food to officers assigned to the blockade points.

> *"People sleep peaceably in their beds at night*
> *only because rough men stand ready*
> *to do violence on their behalf."*
> ~ George Orwell ~

Chapter IX – INDIANA PRELUDE

It is not likely that the Indiana State Police (ISP) would say that John Dillinger was their father, but it was his type that had prompted the Indiana Bankers Association to lobby the legislature for its creation. Eventually, in 1933, the ISP was born. In fact, during its infancy, the first Indiana trooper killed in the line of duty, John Teague, was fatally shot in the hunt for Dillinger.

The ISP and MSP were similar but different. Each prided itself on a rigorous academy and a field training program, things rare in the mid-20th century. Both departments shared the same mission, yet they approached it differently.

Indiana troopers were assigned take-home cruisers, nicknamed "Stripe," likely for the pointed stripe that underlaid the door shield and ran from front to rear. In contrast, they worked from their homes and wore campaign-style hats rather than Michigan's garrison-style caps. Indiana troopers also carried a .38 caliber revolver, but they carried it in a strongside, thumb-break, drop-down holster. This holster sacrificed security for faster drawing. And, whether night or day, Indiana troopers usually patrolled alone.

On the morning of September 30, 1957, Trooper William Kellems drove his Stripe north to Indianapolis with his pretty wife Alice at his side. It is likely that their itinerary had them first meeting family for lunch. He would then leave Alice with them while he went to headquarters for his final oral board, the last hurdle before he could be promoted to trooper first class.

This day had been a long time coming, and it had not been without setback. As he drove, he reminisced about the events that had gotten him to this point.

Kellems had always wanted to be a trooper. But, after graduating from high school, he would first serve in the Air Force and then work for the phone company. In time, he completed the stringent trooper application process which garnered him an invitation to the academy.

He had been among 75 males who had begun the three-month-long recruit school in April 1956. He exceeded the required height of 5-10 and had a medium build. Being a few years older than the median age of the class, Kellems liked to think he presented himself as confident, although some had thought him headstrong and cocky.

As a whole, the class of 1956 proved tougher than most, graduating 73. That created a problem as the ISP only had funding for 50 trooper positions. Kellems was among the 23 that were dismissed. They were assured that as trooper vacancies occurred, they would be filled from that list – that is, as long as it was within a year. Otherwise, their eligibility expired. Deeply disappointed, having resigned from the phone company to go to the academy, he returned home unemployed.

It would not be until November 15 of that year that he would realize his dream, when he was appointed to fill a trooper vacancy at the Charlestown Post. This post was located in south central Indiana and covered six counties. There he would complete his field training and would be assigned to Scott County, located between Indianapolis and Louisville.

Kellems' thoughts now turned to his wife. Both from the Indianapolis area, they had met on a blind date and married ten months later. Alice had emotionally supported him throughout his quest to be a trooper. Three years later, when he was finally accepted to the academy, she waited at home while he completed the three months of training.

Alice Kellems

Picture from TRUE DETECTIVE Jan 1958

With his appointment, the young couple moved to Scottsburg where they rented a small house on South Main Street. In the months that followed, the glamour of being a trooper's wife dimmed as Kellems worked long hours six days a week with ever changing shifts. These stressors began to threaten their marriage. Nevertheless, they did not give up, struggling to make it work.

As Kellems parked his assigned Stripe at headquarters, his thoughts focused on the oral board that awaited him. When the interview was over, he felt confident about how he had represented himself. As he left, he was told he would learn the results by the end of the week.

Kellems then picked up Alice and headed back to Scottsburg. After dropping her off at home, he began his scheduled afternoon shift of patrol, knowing that waiting for the outcome of the oral board would be an anxious time.

As the hours of Monday, September 30, 1957 waned, it grew dark in southern Indiana. The skies clouded, fog formed, and trouble approached.

Chapter X – HOURS 6 - 7 - 8

Not long into Indiana, with Taylor at the wheel, it appears they got lost. When they found themselves in Angola, they couldn't resist stopping at a drive-thru. As they waited for their food, Taylor again checked the Smith & Wesson revolver, the one he had killed the Michigan trooper with, to make sure it was ready for what might come. As he did, the carhop appeared with their food. Quickly he snapped the cylinder shut and concealed it beneath his jacket. He hoped she hadn't seen the gun. If she had, she didn't show it. It would not be until the next day that she would report to authorities her observation.

At some point Whitley resumed driving, his usual assignment, probably because he had a better sense of direction. As they tried to get back on a southern track, they remained alert for the flashing lights that might indicate a roadblock. It was something they so far had been good at avoiding.

At 7:21 p.m. CST, Indiana State Trooper Kellems listened to the Charlestown Post broadcast. "All stations dispatch, concerning the shooting of two Michigan state troopers, and that two subjects possibly in a red-and-white 1955 Buick, Michigan [license plate] KJ2634, may have a woman as a hostage. Car was stolen in Jackson, Michigan, at 4:20 p.m., September 30, 1957."

While this is the broadcast recorded on the ISP radio log, we should not assume that Kellems clearly heard it all. Radio traffic is often broken or other sounds and distractions interfere with it.

Being over 300 miles away, Kellems wondered what the chances were that they would come this way. When he stopped home for a sandwich, he told Alice about it. Having earlier soiled his summer short sleeved uniform shirt, he changed into his winter uniform. Although not the authorized uniform until the next day, he was willing to gamble that he would not see anyone in the next four hours that it matter to, namely a command officer.

After dinner, Kellems then stopped at the home of ISP Detective Sergeant Wayne Tolbert who also resided in Scottsburg. Tolbert is quoted as saying, "Many times he [Kellems] stopped by the house in his off-duty hours to talk about police work. We discussed cases and how they were handled." Tolbert didn't mind the visits; he admired the enthusiasm of the rookie trooper.

It is likely Tolbert suggested that Kellems share the information with the attendants of D & F Garage. It was the 24-hour gas station and repair shop that sat on US-31, the main north-south street in Scottsburg. He pointed out to Kellems that if the duo got this far, they would probably need gas. As Kellems left Tolbert he said, "I'd sure like to get those men. I'm watching for them."

Kellems knew and trusted the D & F Garage night mechanics, Barnie Pruitt and Leonard Hurst were both army veterans and about his own age. Kellems next stopped there and told them about the red-and-white Buick with two white men in it and asked that they call the Charlestown Post if they saw it.

Eventually Whitley drove them to Indiana SR-15, where they regained their sense of direction and turned south. When they passed through Milford, they spotted an abandoned car along the road. They stopped and stole its Indiana license plate, which they bolted over the Buick's rear Michigan plate. Then they removed the Buick's front Michigan license plate and concealed it in a bag in the backseat.

As they accomplished this, Margaret Purdum passed by in her car, not realizing the significance of what she had seen. Later, while she watched the news, she learned a red-and-white Buick was wanted. Wondering if what she had seen might be related, she reported her observations to the South Bend Post of the Indiana State Police. It was 9:19 p.m. CST.

The duo continued south on SR-15 for awhile and then cautiously worked themselves to US-31. They knew if they continued south on it they would eventually cross the Ohio River into Kentucky. Then, with the Michigan border getting farther and farther behind them and a buffer state of Indiana in between, they hoped to become more and more invisible. So far, so good.

In the darkness, Kellems patrolled north on US-31, working his way toward Austin. As he did, he probably thought, "Wouldn't it be something if this was the day I passed my oral board to be advanced to Trooper First Class and arrested two cop killers." The evening wore on.

Paths Crossed: HEART SHOTS

> *"The only thing necessary for the triumph of evil is for good men to do nothing."*
> ~ Edmund Burke ~

Chapter XI – HOUR 9

Trooper Kellems turned on the dome light of his cruiser, a Ford with a manual transmission. He looked at his watch. It was approaching 11:00 p.m. CST. Just an hour remained in his scheduled shift. He remembered that Alice had said she would wait up for him. He pondered the update he had just received over the radio concerning the sighting of a red-and-white Buick in Milford and the possibility they had changed license plates.

Unsure where Milford was, he unfolded his state map to locate it. He could see that Milford was between the Michigan state line and Scottsburg. Although Milford was over 200 miles away, the sighting had been made nearly three hours ago. If it was the duo, it appeared they might be coming his way. If so, they might pass through at any time.

It is likely that Kellems found a spot north of Scottsburg where, like his Michigan counterparts the evening before, he idled his cruiser; its headlights cast across US-31 providing him a glimpse of passing cars' occupants. There, alone in the darkness, the young trooper did not advertise his presence with a flashing red light as those officers manning road blocks did. He watched for the wanted car.

And then, a red-and-white Buick passed by. Kellems quickly shifted his cruiser into gear and pulled onto the highway, not wanting the car to get away. He couldn't be sure it was the wanted Buick, but he planned to find out. He had learned in his short career that frequently when you watch for something, you more often see look-alikes.

Kellems followed the Buick south toward Scottsburg. His headlights silhouetted two persons in the vehicle.

The tailgating car quickly drew the attention of the Buick's driver. Watching his mirror, Whitley realized he was being followed by the police and awakened the dozing Taylor. He did not think he had committed a traffic violation and hoped they were far enough from Michigan that this officer wouldn't be on the lookout for the Buick. If so, perhaps the freshly stolen Indiana license plate would draw them a bye. They decided to turn right off the highway, hoping the patrol car would pass by. It didn't, following instead. While most desperadoes would flee at a time like this, that was not their style.

During the foggy drive led by Whitley, Kellems was eventually able to read the license plate. It was not a Michigan plate which may have made him doubt whether it was the wanted car. He radioed, "Car 11-13 to Charlestown Post, file check [Indiana license plate] RT 1288, red over white 55 Buick, following it west on Moonglo Road, north side of Scottsburg." There was a pause in his transmission as Kellems watched the Buick turn south on South Boatman Road and then east on SR-56.

Unable to radio directly to the Scottsburg police, Kellems continued, "Subjects headed back toward Scottsburg. Have Scottsburg police signal 8 [back me up] at junction of 31 and 56; going to stop the car there." It was 11:06 p.m. CST.

The Charlestown Post then relayed Kellems' request to the Scottsburg police. By now Kellems would have been sure they knew they were being followed by the police, yet they had not fled. Again, he likely wondered if the car might be just a look-alike.

With the patrol car following their every turn, Whitley and Taylor's hope of being invisible evaporated. They sensed what was coming and planned for it. They agreed on what to say and do to draw the trooper in close for their preferred heart shot.

Of their four guns, they decided to use the Mauser. It was the one Whitley had purchased in West Virginia and had been carrying since the first kidnapping of the day. Perhaps, since Taylor had proved himself twice in Michigan, it was Whitley's turn to do likewise in Indiana.

Now the pair unknowingly approached Kellems' designated interception point at the crossroads of 31 and 56, but the Scottsburg Police were nowhere to be seen. The Buick turned south. Kellems followed.

Knowing he would soon exit the perceived safety of the town, Kellems decided to make the stop alone. He activated his red beacon to signal the car to stop. As he did, he glanced to his rearview mirror, hoping to see the Scottsburg Police behind him.

The Buick did not respond, continuing slowly southbound. A block later, Kellems momentarily blurted his siren to get the driver's attention. At the sound of the siren, two things happened.

The Scottsburg police, not knowing that Kellems had already passed through, pulled into the Marathon gas station at the corner of US-31 and SR-56. There they watched for him to come from the west. They did not hear the siren.

Barnie Pruitt, working as a mechanic at D & F Garage, was startled by the siren. It drew his attention to the highway where he saw a two-tone 1955 Buick abruptly stop with a state police cruiser right behind it. Once again, the duo had picked the spot to do battle.

Across the road Pruitt could see two persons in the Buick, illuminated by the street lights. The driver had long, light-colored hair and appeared to be a woman, or perhaps a man wearing a wig. Pruitt recognized Kellems as the trooper who got out of the cruiser.

One can imagine Whitley, wearing a woman's wig, say in a high-pitched voice out his open window, "Is there a problem, officer?" If so, one wonders if this caused Kellems to deduce it was a look-alike and relax his guard. While we cannot know what Kellems was thinking, we will always wonder.

Pruitt watched Kellems walk casually toward the Buick with only his flashlight in hand. Just as Kellems neared the driver's door, Pruitt heard several muffled shots. Kellems staggered back as Pruitt ran toward the Buick, hollering, as he tried to see the license plate. To him, it appeared to be an Indiana plate, but he couldn't read it.

As the Buick began to accelerate away, Kellems drew his revolver as he slumped to a sitting position. Using both hands, he fired five shots at the Buick. Some of the rounds hit the back window, its occupants ducking.

As Kellems fired his last shot, he began to collapse to his side. Pruitt caught his friend. Gently laying him down, he asked, "What happened, Bill?

Kellems gasped, "Call Charlestown; tell them what happened."

Melvin Ray lived nearby and was just getting home when he also heard the shots. Seeing the fallen trooper in front of the patrol car, he too ran to the trooper's aid. Ray arrived just moments after Pruitt, who had been joined by his fellow mechanic, Leonard Hurst.

Turning care of the trooper over to Melvin Ray, Pruitt grabbed Kellems' revolver, and he and Hurst scrambled to the cruiser. At the wheel, Hurst released the parking brake, shifted into first gear, and jerkily sped south in hopes of catching up to the Buick.

As passenger in a darkened cruiser with which he was unfamiliar, Pruitt struggled to find the microphone for the police radio and then make use of it as his dying friend had requested.

It was 11:08 p.m. CST when the Charlestown Post heard over the radio the shocking words, "This is Scottsburg. They have shot Kellems and left him lying in the road. Are going south on 31." The desk officer did not recognize the voice, nor could he get the caller to respond.

Melvin Ray knew Kellems, and on the shadowed street, cared for his friend. He couldn't see much blood, the shifting lights making it difficult to see. Moments later, he was joined by Charles Purkhiser whom he told to go call the police. Meanwhile Ray tried to bring some relief to Kellems' gasping breaths by loosening his gun belt. With that, Kellems went still. Kellems had not lived to learn that he had passed the test to be advanced to Trooper First Class.

Hurst's unfamiliarity with the cruiser's manual transmission made it difficult for him to quickly shift gears to gain speed and overtake the Buick. In the distance, Pruitt thought he saw tail lights turn east on SR-356, but Hurst kept going straight until they got to Underwood. Seeing nothing, they returned to the scene of the shooting, finding the Scottsburg police at Kellems' side.

Lieutenant Robert Bennett was on duty at the Charlestown Post when he learned that Kellems had been shot. He first activated the blockade system, and then he dispatched an ISP detective to the scene. Officers in Scott County and surrounding counties rushed to their assigned points.

ISP Detective Sergeant Wayne Tolbert, living within a block of the shooting, arrived at the scene at 11:25 p.m. It was difficult for him to believe that Kellems, who had just visited him a few hours earlier, lay before him in the southbound lane shot dead. It was surreal.

Tolbert briefly interviewed witnesses and arranged for the scene to be protected. Then, in the company of Scott County Sheriff Ralph Morris, he sadly went to the nearby Kellems home to advise Alice of her husband's death.

Alice probably thought the noise from the porch was Bill coming home from work. The knocks at the door seemed odd, and when she opened it, she was surprised to see Detective Tolbert and Sheriff Morris. As gently as possible, in so many words, they told her that her husband would never be coming home.

Alice turned to look at the picture on the wall. It was of Bill, standing proudly beside his assigned Stripe. She may have thought that their last day together had been a good one that had ended badly. Taking the picture from the wall, she now clutched it as she sat on the couch and quietly wept.

Indiana Trooper William Kellems

Source of picture unknown

Later on, Detective Tolbert examined the deceased trooper's body for evidence as it rested at the L. B. Stewart Funeral Home in Scottsburg. He noted two bullet holes. One passed through Kellems' uniform tie, through the long-sleeve winter uniform shirt where the buttons fasten, and then through a heavy undershirt before penetrating skin in the center of his chest. The second bullet hole was found in Kellems' right upper arm, about three inches below the shoulder.

Tolbert probably thought, "Mortally wounded and his right arm injured, Kellems returned fire." The bullet that had passed through his heart was found lodged beneath Kellems' left shoulder blade. It was a copper-coated .32 caliber bullet and was later matched to the Mauser.

Among the officers activated to man a blockade point in reference to the shooting of Kellems was 29-year-old Trooper Robert Pond, a three-year veteran of the force. Pond was assigned to Jennings County, which was located northeast of Scott County.

Indiana Trooper Robert Pond

Picture from TRUE DETECTIVE – Jan 1958

Like many times before, the point Pond was assigned was at the intersection of SR-3 and SR-7. Having no partner and needing a backup, he telephoned Charles Dudley, the second-term, 47-year-old sheriff of Jennings County. As most rural sheriffs did in that era, the sheriff lived at the combination office, jail, and residence.

One can imagine the context of the call. Pond, sensing he had awakened Dudley, said "Sheriff, it's Pond. Can you back me on manning a blockade point?"

"I suppose, but you know tomorrow is my 25th wedding anniversary."

"You know Trooper Kellems in Scottsburg?" Pond didn't wait for an answer. "He just got shot and killed. I'll be right over to pick you up."

"I'll be ready." The sheriff quickly put on his uniform.

The sheriff and his deputy, Clyde Perkins, shared a phone line and the deputy had listened in on the call. Perkins, living a distance away, got ready to go, perhaps to relieve the sheriff so that he might be rested to celebrate his anniversary the next day.

Sheriff Dudley was waiting at the street, shotgun in hand, when Pond pulled up in his cruiser. The drive from the jail to their blockade point was not far.

As he drove, Pond briefed Dudley on what had happened and the descriptions of the wanted car and suspects. Pond then said something like, "Sheriff, it seems like we've done this a dozen times, but this time we are going to do it a little differently. Rather than posting at the intersection of SR-3 and SR-7, we're going to go around the curve and post at the south end of the Vernon bridge. That way, if they come, they'll be on top of us before they know it. I'll stand in the road and check traffic; you cover me."

Earlier that day, Whitley and Taylor had applied their contingency plans – previously only imagined – with amazing effectiveness. They would now look to repeat them, knowing they needed to do a double-back and get another getaway car.

Racing south from shooting the trooper in Scottsburg, Whitley turned east at the first paved road he saw, SR-356. A few miles later they completed their double-back when they turned north on SR-3.

Nora Nichols was driving with her sister-in-law, her 28-month-old adopted Korean orphan, and her six-week-old baby. The car was headed back to Ohio. They had just spent a long weekend visiting her sister-in-law's husband, a soldier at Fort Knox, Kentucky. It was late and ground fog was forming in the lowlands as they traveled the lonely highway.

As she drove north on SR-3, a car came up behind her fast, flashing its lights. Twice it pulled alongside her, both times on a double yellow line. The third time, the car forced her to a stop on the side of the road, pulling to the shoulder in front of her. In her headlights, she saw a short, pudgy man step from the passenger side and hurry back to her car. As he did, she quickly locked her doors.

The man grabbed her door handle to open it. Finding it locked, he said, "We're the state police, we want to see your driver's license."

Nichols didn't believe him, but she did roll down her window a little bit and said, "All right, just a minute." With that, the man looked away. When he did, Nichols stomped on the gas pedal, spinning tires as she swerved around the red-and-white Buick and sped north. She would later say that she was surprised her action hadn't jerked the man's hand off.

Undoubtedly infuriated by being beaten at his own ploy, Taylor jumped back in the Buick, and Whitley raced after the car. Courageously, the defiant Nichols now drove 80-90 mph into the foggy darkness. With the Buick chasing right behind her, she hoped to make it to the next town where she might find the police.

Looking back, it appears it was Nichols' brave action that

began to change the tide of momentum between good and evil.

"Who dares, wins."
Motto of the British Special Air Service

Nora Nichols

Compliments of Rhonda Lippencott, daughter of Nora Nichols

> *"Excellence is to do a common thing*
> *in an uncommon way."*
> ~ Booker T. Washington ~

Chapter XII – HOUR 10

Trooper Pond parked his cruiser, its red beacon flashing, by a vegetable trailer on the west side of the road, just south of what locals called the Vernon bridge. The bridge crossed the Vernon Fork of the Muscatatuck River. He positioned it perpendicular, headlights shining across the highway so it would illuminate what would soon be his post. Before leaving the security of the idling car, he gazed out the window at his surroundings. The circumstances, coupled with the darkness and drifting fog, gave the midnight hour an eerie atmosphere.

As Sheriff Dudley surveyed the adjustment to the blockade point, he agreed with Pond's change. Traffic would not see the blockade until they were upon them. If there was a perfect location for a blockade, this might be it.

Settled, Pond opened his car door and strolled to the center of the road. With his shotgun held at port arms, he checked cars. Dudley, standing beside the patrol car, watched with his shotgun at the ready. They kidded back and forth to ease the tension.

The third motorist Pond contacted was Nora Nichols, who was stunned by the sudden appearance of the police. Frantically she said, "The two men in the Buick! They've been following us. They forced us off the road twice and tried to take the car! They're right behind us."

"All right, get out of here fast," Pond snapped. He stepped back, trying to escape the next car's blinding headlights. As he did, he called to Dudley, "Watch it. I believe that's it."

Caught up in the pursuit of the fleeing woman, Whitley likely cursed himself for having chased her into the blockade, the first one he had been unable to avoid. The manner in which the trooper stepped back from her car suggested Whitley had also just lost the element of surprise. Luring the trooper in close, followed by a distraction, would have to be foregone. He would have to attempt a longer heart shot than preferred. Quickly pointing the Mauser pistol out his open window, Whitley fired. His aim was true.

With that shot, a firestorm was unleashed between good and evil. Whether spite or accident, bullets struck Nichols' back window as she sped away, fortunately injuring no one. It was likely Taylor who fired these bullets from his Smith & Wesson revolver.

Whitley continued to fire the Mauser until it jammed. He and Taylor then abandoned their primary firearms, dropping them on the front floorboard of the Buick. Counting the jammed round, the Mauser would later be found to contain four cartridges. The Smith & Wesson held two live cartridges. The duo now switched to their second guns with Taylor using the Colt and Whitley using the Savage.

Had Pond not been holding the shotgun at port arms, it is likely Whitley's shot would have been fatal to the heart. In that position, Pond's right hand grasped the stock of the shotgun that lay across the center of his chest. Penetrating Pond's right hand, the bullet was unable to pass through the wood stock where it became embedded. In a time prior to bullet-resistant vests, the stock had proved a worthy substitute.

With a mangled hand, Pond retaliated by emptying the shotgun on the Buick, its buckshot stalling the car and perforating the windshield. Dudley immediately joined the firefight, his buckshot blasting the driver's door in an attempt to kill the shooter.

Stolen Buick of Dorothea LeCronier

From FALLEN TROOPERS OF THE M.S.P. – V. BECK

As Taylor and Whitley scrambled to exit the passenger side of the car, away from the officers, pellets ripped into the Buick, the only ones penetrating being through the glass. Miraculously, Whitley was only struck in the thumb. At least fifteen of the pellets found their way to Taylor's side and upper arm. But like Pond, neither showed a hint of an injury.

When their shotguns ran dry, Pond and Dudley transitioned to their .38 caliber revolvers. Whether a planned diversion or not, the Buick now slowly rolled back across the road toward the cruiser. As it did, Dudley paused from the shootout to quickly use the state police radio to contact the Seymour Post, saying, "We're shooting it out with them now."

Dudley then sneaked to the empty vegetable trailer that sat beside the cruiser, revolver in hand. From there he spotted Taylor, creeping alongside the slowly rolling Buick as it neared the cruiser, using it for cover. He could see that Taylor's attention was on Pond, who now fired from the kneeling position in the ditch. Secluded in the dark, Dudley waited for a clear shot, and then took it.

Seeing the flash of the gun and hearing its crack, Taylor now turned his fire to Dudley. Then, as if taking turns, one at a time, they emptied their guns at each other. With each shot, both probably expected the other to fall, but neither did.

In the exchange of gunfire, Taylor was hit with .38 caliber bullets in one, maybe both shoulders, but he was yet to show it. Meanwhile Pond and Whitley were firing their guns at each other.

With his gun empty, Dudley cursed himself. In his rush to the blockade, he had brought no extra ammunition for either the shotgun or five-shot snub-nosed revolver.

Suddenly, the duo abandoned their attack. Their likely intent to kill the officers and take their patrol car changed to a retreat when their handguns became spent.

With empty guns, Dudley was resisting panic when he heard Pond yell, "They're running across the bridge." As he heard those words, the shot-up Buick rolled to a stop against the cruiser. Pond and Dudley rushed to the cruiser's glovebox where extra ammunition was stowed.

As Taylor ran north across the bridge, he began to limp, his wounds beginning to take their toll. Whitley, wanting to avoid the exposure of the road, hopped the guard rail to run beneath the bridge, wading across the shallow stream. Both kept their pistols in hand, although neither was likely operable.

On the other side of the bridge, William Mason and his friend, James Lane, were sitting in their Dodge. They had been driving south from Illinois when they saw the flashing red light and a car across the road. Initially thinking the road was blocked because of an accident they stopped, their car stalling. Then they saw two men, one noticeably older than the other, shooting toward the police car.

As Mason hurriedly tried to restart his Dodge, his attention focused on the instrument panel, he did not see the older man limping across the bridge. Lane, his passenger, did, jumping from the car and running away.

James Lane and William Mason

Picture from OFFICIAL DETECTIVE – Jan 1958

When Whitley returned to the road on the north side of the bridge, he saw Taylor at the driver's door of a Dodge. There, he rejoined him.

Two armed men stood at Mason's car door before he could follow his friend's lead. "Scoot over," Taylor growled as he opened the driver's door and slid in. Now behind the wheel, the bleeding Taylor threatened, "Do as you are told or I will kill yah."

It was now Taylor who tried to start the stalled car. On his fifth try, another car pulled up tight to the Dodge's rear bumper.

At age 47, the quiet-spoken Clyde Perkins had been the sheriff's deputy for seven years. Overhearing the phone call that Pond had earlier made to the sheriff, he put on his uniform and strapped on his gun belt. Being a southpaw, he carried his weapon on his left side. Like the sheriff, he only took his .38 caliber, 5-shot, snub-nosed revolver.

From home, he headed south in his police car. As Perkins drove, he was unaware of the firefight that was now in progress.

He could not have heard the sheriff use the state police radio to call the Seymour Post from the bridge, as the two agencies used different radio frequencies.

It was supposed to have been North Vernon Patrolman Lester Kenens' day off, but he was filling in for another officer who had taken the night off. While on patrol, he noticed Deputy Perkins' unmarked police car going south through North Vernon, and he began following it. As he did, he was waved down by the frantic Nora Nichols, whom Trooper Pond had told a minute earlier, "All right, get out of here fast,"

Deputy Perkins, unaware of what was happening either behind or before him, continued on, while Nichols excitedly told Kenens what had just happened. First learning of the shootout, Kenens was anxious to get there, but experience reminded him to quickly check her car to make sure the villains were not concealed inside it. Done, he then raced for the bridge.

Bridge over the Vernon Fork of the Muscatatuck River

As Perkins approached the bridge from the north side, he saw a stalled Dodge displaying Illinois license plates in the southbound lane. Assuming it was stalled and needed pushed off the roadway, he pulled his car up tight, just touching the two bumpers. He then got out of his car to see how the bumpers had matched. Seeing that they needed an adjustment, Perkins got back into his unmarked police car.

As Taylor and Whitley watched Perkins from inside the stalled Dodge, they realized the officer was oblivious to what was going on. With that, they recognized an opportunity.

Just as Perkins seated himself in his car, Whitley jumped out of the Dodge and walked back to Perkins' door. Perkins was shocked when Whitley pointed a pistol at his head and said, "You dirty son of a bitch cop. Put your hands up or I'll kill you."

As Whitley ordered Perkins from the car, Taylor joined them, whispering into Perkins' ear, "I've already killed one dirty son of a bitch cop today and one more won't make a goddam difference. . . I have three bullets in me and one more won't make a difference. You better give up your gun."

As Taylor whispered, Whitley was able to quickly disarm Perkins of his revolver from his fast-draw holster. Whitley then pushed Perkins back into his car, sliding into the driver's seat beside him.

Taylor ran around the car to the passenger side to get in. As he did, another car pulled in behind them. Heads turned, revealing a marked police car. Perkins figured it would be his huge friend, North Vernon Patrolman Lester Kenens. Like Michigan Trooper Pellot's nickname Cochise, his friend's nickname also contrasted with his appearance. Perkins yelled to him, "Tiny, go back; they have my gun and have taken me hostage."

Patrolman Lester "Tiny" Kenens

Compliments of Brian Taylor, grandson of Lester Kenens

Whether Kenens did not hear Perkins' warning or just ignored it is not known. What is known is that Kenens kept coming.

From inside Perkins' police car, Whitley turned and fired all the rounds at Kenens from the revolver he had taken from Perkins. He shot through the back window. One bullet struck Kenens in the chest, a shot which lodged beside his heart. Another round struck the third finger on his right hand.

Badly wounded, Kenens remained stalwart as he returned fire. One of his six shots struck Taylor in the right temple. Dropping his Colt pistol to the pavement, Taylor collapsed into the right front seat of Perkins' commandeered police car.

The large girth of Kenens' chest, combined with the diminished velocity of the .38 caliber round after breaking through the car's rear window, prevented the bullet from penetrating Kenens' big heart. Becoming faint, Kenens retreated back to his patrol car to summon aid.

Whitley now held the gun to Perkins' head and ordered him to put his head on Whitley's right leg, covering his head with his fedora-type sheriff hat. In the melee, Perkins had not counted the rounds that Whitley had fired. If he had, he would have known the gun was now empty.

Using his right hand to hold the gun to Perkins' temple, his thumb bleeding onto Perkins' head, Whitley drove with his left. When he took off, the passenger door swung shut, but Taylor's feet, hanging out the door, kept it from latching. Whether another double-back maneuver or a forced choice, Whitley headed south. He would again have to navigate the gauntlet which he had just survived.

As Pond and Dudley hurriedly reloaded their guns, they heard the shooting on the other side of the bridge. They then recognized Perkins' police car crossing the bridge and accelerating toward them. As it did, they heard someone (probably Mason or Lane) yell, "They got the deputy hostage." Holding their fire, they watched the car roar by.

Whitley turned the deputy's car right on SR-3. His head down and covered, Perkins could not see anything. But knowing the area, he tried to trace in his mind the route they traveled. As he lie there, head on Whitley's lap, barrel pressed against his temple, he felt warm sticky blood. He didn't think it was his. He then heard a gasp from the dead weight that leaned on his right side. It was Taylor's final sound.

As Whitley raced through a curve to the left, the unlatched car door swung open, allowing centrifugal force to pull Taylor's body from the car. It tumbled down the roadway, coming to rest on the edge of SR-3. Whitley didn't pause.

Pond and Dudley scrambled into the state police cruiser to give chase. As Pond steered his car away from the Buick that was pressed against it, Dudley radioed the Seymour Post, "The suspects are headed south on 3, and we are gonna try to catch them." Dudley worried he would never again see his deputy alive.

As they rounded the first curve to the left, the cruiser's headlights illuminated a body on the side of the road. Dudley yelled, "My God! Stop Bob! There's Clyde."

Bob Pond swerved, nearly hitting the body, screeching to a stop beyond it. In the darkness, they ran back to check what they feared would be Clyde Perkins. They were relieved to see what their flashlights illuminated.

With Taylor ejected from the car, Whitley then turned right at the next dirt road and drove a short distance. He then turned around, driving back toward SR-3, his headlights extinguished. He stopped the car a distance back from SR-3 and waited.

Leaving the body on the side of the road, Pond and Dudley jumped back into the cruiser and raced south, hoping to spot Perkin's fleeing police car. As they did, Dudley noticed that Pond was driving with only his left hand; his right rested on the seat in a pool of blood. Dudley said, "Bob, you're hurt."

"I'm okay, I can keep driving," Pond answered.

Seeing the cruiser speed south on SR-3, Whitley now idled his darkened car nearer the road so he could better tell if other traffic was approaching. Hearing and seeing nothing, he crossed the pavement and continued east on the dirt road. Eventually he made his way to SR-7 where he turned south.

Dudley again radioed the Seymour Post, updating them with their findings and telling them of Pond's wound. As he did, they met a state police cruiser coming north. Their cars facing in opposite directions, they stopped on the roadway to exchange information. Neither had seen the carjacked police car.

About that time, the Seymour Post radioed Trooper Pond,

ordering him to immediately seek medical attention. With many troopers converging on the area, Pond returned Dudley to the sheriff's office and then drove himself to the hospital.

Dudley then got in his sheriff's car and picked up his friend and colleague, North Vernon Police Chief Vernard Rice. They now joined the hunt for Perkins and for the criminal that had kidnapped him and then shot Kenens.

Being in the sheriff's car, they shared radio frequencies with Perkins' car and the North Vernon police, but not with the state police. At the confluence of SR-3 and SR-7, they met another state police cruiser. They were told they had just checked SR-3 and had seen nothing. Dudley decided to drive down SR-7.

Into the fog of the night, Whitley now drove south on SR-7. In short order he met a convoy of state police cruisers racing north. He watched his mirror. Power turns followed brake lights and then headlights began to rapidly close in on him.

The day's events suggest that trying to outrun a police car was not part of their contingency plans, nor was surrender. Whitley turned into a driveway and stopped. Not wanting to leave Perkins with his revolver, he tossed it into the darkness.

In his pocket was his last remaining gun, the Savage pistol, the one that had shot Trooper Vogel. Although jammed, he had kept it; perhaps he hoped to make it operable or use it to bluff.

Once again, Whitley created a diversion by leaving the car so it would roll backward as he disappeared into the foggy woods. Perkins lay on the seat, fearing that Whitley waited outside the door and would kill him if he raised his head.

State Police cruisers quickly surrounded the stolen deputy's car, as it now slowly rolled backward to a stop. Troopers exited their cars, guns at the ready. None wanted to be the third trooper to be killed that day because of hesitancy.

Perkins, seeing the flashing red lights, now felt it safe to raise his head. When he did another firestorm erupted. Perkins ducked and then pressed his body onto the front floorboard, the microphone close at hand. Earlier police bullets had failed to penetrate doors to hit Taylor and Whitley. That deficiency would now save Perkins.

As Dudley drove south, as if the voice of a ghost, he heard Perkins' quavering voice over the radio, "Car Eleven, they're shooting at me."

Dudley floored the gas pedal as he quickly switched the radio to two-way and asked, "Where are you?"

"I don't know," Perkins answered.

Realizing what was going on, Chief Rice grabbed the microphone from Sheriff Dudley and radioed his own station. He told the dispatcher to telephone the Seymour Post and have them radio their troopers and order them to quit shooting the deputy's car.

During the time that it took for this to be relayed, troopers continued to fire. Having just survived being killed by criminals, Perkins now feared death from police bullets.

As Dudley crested the hill, he saw Perkins' car illuminated by a ring of state police cruisers. Nearly colliding with one, he skidded to a stop. The air, fouled with the odor of burned gunpowder, was now joined with the stench of scorched brakes and tires. Dudley jumped from his car, yelling, "Stop shooting." Suddenly it became quiet, ears ringing in protest of the sudden silence.

Dudley exclaimed, "That's my deputy in that car." A trooper countered that as a hostage, perhaps the deputy was being forced to radio he was alone to lure them in so his captor could make another kill. It was suggested they push one of the state police cruisers ahead of them for cover to get closer.

When they got within ten feet of Perkins' bullet-riddled car, they stopped and ordered him out. Cautiously, Perkins raised his grey-haired head, now soaked in the blood that had oozed from

Whitley's shot thumb. With no shots fired, he opened the door and stepped out. Seeing his sheriff, he pointed at the troopers and angrily said, "They were shooting at me."

The sheriff consoled Perkins. "No matter, it's over. You're safe now."

In Michigan, it was about 1:00 a.m. Ten hours had elapsed since Michigan Trooper Doug Vogel had begun to expose Victor Whitley and Ralph Taylor as the criminals they were. The first and last hour had been the costliest.

Chapter XIII – OVERTIME

As Whitley ran blindly into the tangled thicket, he could feel the pocketed Savage pistol bouncing against his thigh. In the foggy darkness, he could see nothing to guide his flight other than the police lights he fled. Without them, he probably would have unwittingly circled back to his start.

In short order he began to gasp for air, as his panicked flight had put him into oxygen debt. And then the shooting began. Instinctively he dropped to the ground while he tried to understand it. Were the police shooting wildly in his direction? By the time the shooting stopped, his breaths were more measured. He cautiously stood up, looking and listening. Sensing nothing, he now paced his escape. He tried to stay on an eastward course, creeping through woods, fields, and thickets as quietly as possible.

As he did, he began to consider the magnitude of the day and his dwindling options. Ralph Taylor in his evil mind probably felt like he had gone down in a blaze of glory like his hero John Dillinger. For certain Taylor had fulfilled his prophecy; he wouldn't be going back to prison.

Whitley wondered what fate held for him. He was pretty sure that he remained a John Doe to the police. If he could just get away, he might be able to continue a life of freedom by his birth name. Becoming Louis L. Schick was no longer an option. Those credentials had been left behind when they abandoned the stolen Buick during the shootout at the Muscatatuck River bridge.

Perhaps he would find an unlocked car, a security-lax farmer having left his keys in it. Or, just maybe, he would jump a slow-moving train passing through the nearby countryside and be able to vanish from the area.

After the report of the sighting in Milford where the license

97

plate was taken, MSP and ISP kept an open phone line. At 12:40 a.m. EST, MSP learned of the murder of Trooper Kellems in Scottsburg. As they radioed the sad update to the weary Michigan troopers on blockade points, they were told to stay vigilant; the pair might double back.

Like in Michigan, funeral homes in rural Indiana provided both hearse and ambulance services. Upon graduation from mortician school, young Jerry Sharp moved from northern Indiana to North Vernon to work at the well-established Dowd Funeral Home. In time, he became the operations manager for the aging Mr. and Mrs. Dowd. A part of his duties was for him and his assistant to answer calls for service in the off-hours.

During the early hours of October 1, Sharp answered a phone call directing him to SR-3, south of SR-7, to pick up a body from the road. Like most first responders, he wondered what he would find and what the story was that went with it.

The body wasn't hard to find. Like a star actor in a Broadway play, it had all the spotlights directed at it, except they were aimed by troopers, not stagehands.

There Sharp collected the body of a middle-aged white man who appeared to have been shot several times, although it was hard to tell for certain in the oblique lighting. Having loaded the body in the hearse, he began his return drive to the funeral home. Looking in his rearview mirror, Sharp realized he was leading a parade of state police cruisers.

Once there, officers followed him into the funeral home. It was more state police than he had ever seen in one place. Not only did they want to examine the body, but they wanted to make the funeral home into a temporary command post. Having a large parking lot, briefing room, bathrooms, offices, and a location near the scene of the ongoing manhunt, the funeral home would make a good one, he supposed.

The commotion awakened the hard-of-hearing Mr. Dowd who

lived on the second floor of the establishment. He came down the stairs in his robe to investigate. With his permission, troopers began to carry in all kinds of gear. Having thought he had seen everything, Mr. Dowd made an addition to his list and then returned to his bed.

Like the MSP on the day before, the ISP had several crime scenes to process. A part of that was the dead body that Sharp now laid on the embalming table.

From the pocket of the pants worn by the body, detectives removed a billfold. Perhaps it would reveal who lay dead before them. In it they found driver's licenses for Ralph Taylor and Victor Whitley. The name Ralph Taylor had been earlier provided to them by the MSP as a suspect in the shooting of their troopers. The description on the license matched that of the dead body, the height being the most noteworthy. The name Victor Whitley was new to them, its description different from the dead body. They then counted $560 in cash, mostly in fifty and hundred-dollar bills.

Also tucked in the billfold was an army discharge card in the name of Ralph Taylor, dated September 28, 1945. Reading the card, the detective wondered if Taylor's military training and World War II experiences had played a part in his behavior this day.

Detectives noted three wounds to the head. The one to the left temple could have also made an exit hole. The third, which was not as fresh, was more of a crease. (This wound would later be credited to MSP Sergeant O'Donnell as a grazing shot he fired just after MSP Trooper Pellot was killed.) There was also a bullet hole in each shoulder. They appeared to have been made by .38 caliber rounds. On Taylor's right side and upper arm, there were at least 15 shotgun pellet holes. There would be no autopsy of Taylor, the county seeing no good reason to justify such an expense.

Amid the chaos, Sharp was asked to return to the scene to look for Kenens who was believed to have been shot, his whereabouts then unknown. During Sharp's search, it was learned that Kenens was at the Seymour Hospital.

About that time, Sharp came across a trooper that asked him to park his ambulance on SR-3, red lights flashing, and stop traffic. Once the cars stopped, the trooper said he would come from the darkened ditch and contact the driver to make sure the wanted criminal wasn't in the car.

Not long into this task, Sharp realized that was not his job and that he was putting himself in danger. Sharp then excused himself and returned to his duties in the safety of the funeral home.

Another set of investigators had the stolen Buick towed to a nearby garage where they searched it for evidence. Among other things, they discovered the black Samsonite satchel which contained the identities of Cecil Compeau and Louis Schick, the documents' purpose now thwarted.

As troopers from around the state arrived, ISP sergeants, unfamiliar with the area, conferred with Sheriff Dudley and Deputy Perkins on how to best utilize troopers to form a perimeter. In their analysis, they agreed it was likely the suspect had fled east, but to be safe they would cordon off a 10-acre section of woods and soybean fields.

When ISP Captain Nelson and Lieutenant Dillon arrived from headquarters in Indianapolis, they assumed command of the ground search for the criminal, now only known as John Doe. After being briefed, they privately conferred outside the ring of light.

They returned to the group and announced their decision to wait until daybreak to begin a ground search. They hoped the threat had been contained. If it had, time was on their side. To search now, in the dark, would be more dangerous and less thorough. ISP Major Paul T. Beverforden later arrived and took overall command of the manhunt.

Deputy Clyde Perkins and Sheriff Charles Dudley

Compliments of the North Vernon Plain Dealer

By 2:30 a.m., it appeared there were at least 175 troopers on location, with more arriving. As the troopers reported for assignment, they talked among themselves, sharing what they had heard. With five officers shot in the chest, the suspects appeared to have trained to shoot for the heart. Some referred to them as the "heart shooters."

With the reinforcements, they tightened the cordon. If the perimeter had trapped the criminal, they didn't want it to be sprung.

But, in case he had slipped through, residents within a 15-mile radius were aroused and warned. Officers made sure their parked cars were keyless and locked.

Additionally, in the event John Doe had stolen a car and left ahead of the net being cast, like they had somehow done in Michigan, troopers hoped he would be caught in one of the blockade points that spanned a 50-mile radius.

Knightstown Marshal Guy Fausset and his bloodhound were summoned in hopes that Princess could track down the criminal. But the scene was too flooded with human scent for her to be of any service. Furthermore, the dense fog prevented helicopters from being of any use.

Princess, Marshal Fausset, and unknown trooper

Compliments of the Indianapolis Star

Anxious to begin, troopers were told of the plan. About 5:00 a.m., they began to form a 300-yard skirmish line consisting of a hundred or more troopers spaced only feet apart. With a few walkie-talkies, a rare commodity for that era, they hoped to maintain the integrity of an eastward wave. Each trooper, campaign-style hat on head, shotgun in hand, galoshes on feet, anxiously awaited daylight and the order to begin.

The planners of the daybreak search had been right, Whitley had fled east. He had painstakingly worked himself through woods, soybean fields, and thickets. In the darkness he had been unable to make the jammed pistol operable. And, try as he might, he had been unable to sneak through the police-lined perimeter.

As the night grew long, Whitley became tired and hungry, and his wounded thumb now throbbed in pain. Once again he wondered what his own fate might be. Miserable and with his partner dead, his determination to escape began to fade.

He pondered his options, recalling that the only way two people can keep a secret is if one is dead. He decided to give up. He would cooperate, and in doing so paint Taylor as the villain and himself as the victim.

He certainly did not want to be found with any gun, let alone the Savage pistol that had been used to shoot a Michigan trooper. He tossed it in a creek, hoping to have washed his hands of it. (It would not be until the following Sunday that a trooper using a metal-detecting device recovered it. The pistol was determined to be jammed because the magazine had been loaded with a mixture of similarly sized .32 caliber and .380 caliber ammunition.)

Whitley believed that the police would jump at the chance to kill him. He mentally reviewed the various contingency plans he and Taylor had previously conjured up, finding none that were fitting for his situation. Now alone, he began to envision how he might surrender in a manner that would make it hard for the police to justify killing him.

While minutes felt like hours, he began to shiver as time slowly passed during the chilly night. Over and over he reviewed how he might try to influence his surrender to his favor.

His thoughts were interrupted when, in the far distance, he

heard the whistle of a slow-moving train, now a missed opportunity. Little did he know, the perceived option would have been for nought as two police officers rode the train, hoping he would jump aboard.

He could not know that an acquaintance he had made that very night would be his saving grace in the years to come, that is, if you call a hostage an acquaintance. Looking back, one wonders if this was an example of a psychological condition that in 1973 would be labeled the Stockholm Syndrome. In it, the hostage bonds with their captor.

And while Whitley shivered, the family of NVPD Patrolman "Tiny" Kenens slept. That is until they were awakened by a loud knocking at the front door of their home. Leaving their infant brother to sleep in the crib, four sisters, all under the age of eleven, followed their mother to the door. They waited on the stair case as they watched her open it. There stood Officer Wally Lehigh who they knew. He said, "June, Tiny has been shot, it looks bad. You better get to the hospital." The girls screamed hysterically.

Finally Sergeant William Thompson deemed it light enough. He ordered the eager troopers to begin their forward movement and maintain a line the best the terrain would allow. Over the next two hours, the wave of troopers passed through two heavily wooded sectors, two damp soybean fields, and crossed the fences that separated them.

Indiana troopers searching for fugitive

Picture from TRUE DETECTIVE – Jan 1958

In the silence of the early morning light, Whitley first heard the searchers coming. He peeked through the foliage to see three officers approaching his lair. With hands on his head, he stood and whistled.

While every officer in the line hoped they would be the one who found the killer, the whistle was heard by ISP officers Gray, Kirkland, and Lee. Looking to the whistle, they saw against the skyline the silhouette of a man standing on the knoll. With guns drawn, they moved in to claim their prize. It was 7:15 a.m. CST

Stoically he stood erect, hands on his head, chin high, and appearing defiant. His face was scratched with blood smeared about him and clothes torn. He dared not move. He knew any move could be fatal.

Once handcuffed, he was searched. On his person they found $390. Like the stash found on the body of his comrade, it was mostly in larger bills. When asked, he said his name was Victor Wayne Whitley and he was from Texas. Finally, the mystery man had a name. He was escorted back to where a police transport vehicle waited.

And with him, a pack of troopers hustled back to the staging point, wanting to get a glimpse of the quarry each had hunted and hoped to capture. Recognizing that the first step toward closure for his troopers was actually laying eyes on the villain, Major Beverforden grasped the handcuffed Whitley by the shoulder and paraded him before the line of troopers.

Along with the scores of troopers had come a mob of reporters who recognized a photographic opportunity. Bulbs flashed. In print, a reporter described Whitley as being a "tall, broad-shouldered, handsome youth."

Victor Whitley and ISP officer

Compliments of the North Vernon Plain Dealer

Whitley had no illusions of getting off scot-free. He planned to cooperate, and in doing so influence the outcome in his favor. He knew Taylor would be happy to take all the blame. Whitley hoped to avoid execution, and who knows, maybe one day again be a free man. He was then whisked off to the Seymour Post for an interview.

At 8:38 a.m., an ISP captain reported to the MSP the killing of Ralph Taylor and the apprehension of the second suspect, his name being Victor Wayne Whitley. Finally, weary troopers were released in both Michigan and Indiana to go home.

Whitley waited patiently in the interview room of the Seymour Post. While he did, detectives tried to determine what would have caused the duo to rage such violence. ISP and MSP detectives exchanged information over the telephone in an effort to determine a motive.

The ISP learned from the MSP that the dead Ralph Taylor was from West Virginia and wanted for parole violation. All they knew about Victor Whitley was that he was a Texan. They had been unable to find any criminal record for him.

The detectives had answers to the who, what, where, when, and how. The one they couldn't answer was why. They hoped Whitley would tell them.

Heinous cases, especially when the suspect was believed to have killed a fellow officer, test an interviewer's acting ability. Like the generations of detectives before them, and those that would follow, they knew that a civil, casual opening to the interview most often created an atmosphere conducive to a confession. It was a time to build the rapport they hoped would allow the truth to be told. Not having a clue to what precipitated such violent behavior, they decided to open with a general approach.

Having allowed Whitley to stew, ISP Detectives Hertzing and Bufkin now entered the room and took their seats. When they had settled, a few moments of silence reigned before the lead interviewer said in a friendly tone, "What have you been doing for the past few months?" And with it, the sparring of the interview began.

It was the type of question Whitley had hoped for. Remaining stoic, he shrugged his shoulders and said, "Oh, just pulling armed robberies." The door had just been opened for him to gain their trust. He added that until yesterday, they had never fired a gun.

Whitley readily outlined his and Taylor's nationwide four-month robbery spree. Amazingly, he recalled twenty-one heists, the town and state where they were committed, and sometimes the amount of loot. Robberies were the least of Whitley's worries, and he realized his admission to them might earn him some credibility.

The detectives listened and took notes. Feeling the subject adequately covered, they then turned the focus toward the ten hours of violence. It was the elephant in the room that they hoped Whitley would illuminate.

Whitley tried to distance himself from the shooting of the officers. The Michigan part was easy, the Indiana side not so much. Probably because two of his victims had survived and would point to him, he admitted to shooting Trooper Pond and Patrolman Kenens. He tried to minimize his involvement, saying that it wasn't until the bridge that his finger touched the trigger. That was a premise he would always maintain except for one known written exception made years later.

The spotlight then turned to the murder of Trooper Kellems. Whitley told detectives that it was Taylor who had pulled the trigger. He described that when they stopped for the Indiana trooper, Taylor told him to distract the trooper by leaning back in the driver's seat so that he could easily reach around and shoot him.

Whitley was pretty sure that other than Taylor or Kellems who were now dead, no one would have been in a position to see who had fired the shot killing the trooper. If Whitley had been wearing a wig, possibly left in the car by the owner, a drama teacher, there was no mention of it in the report of this interview.

Very possibly, in the fast-paced developments, Detectives

Hertzing and Bufkin were unaware of witness Barnie Pruitt's observation that the driver of the Buick, when Kellems was shot was either a woman with long hair or a man wearing a wig. Nor was a wig recorded to have been found in the Buick when it was inventoried by the police. Of course, there would have been ample opportunity for the wig to have been discarded while Whitley and Taylor fled Scottsburg toward Vernon.

Throughout the interview, Whitley presented himself as dull, unemotional, and totally dominated by Ralph Taylor. This portrayal was supported by him saying that Taylor kept the guns until just before a robbery, at which time Whitley would be issued the Mauser. He also said that Taylor even kept his driver's license with his own. With that statement, the detectives glanced to each other with a nod, now understanding why his license had been found in Taylor's billfold.

Whitley continued to answer questions but volunteered only information that was to his benefit. While he described Taylor as being very controlling, when asked if they had an intimate relationship, he denied it.

By now, all occupants of the interview room were exhausted, particularly Whitley who had just survived an intense 24 hours. Whitley's statement answered the why by painting Taylor as the evil one, an essentially vicious and violent man. Whitley was then driven to Scottsburg where he was arraigned before the justice of the peace on the charge of murder and then jailed.

Firearms identification would later show that Trooper Kellems was killed with the Mauser. Admittedly, Whitley had been carrying the Mauser before Kellems was shot, and admittedly he shot Trooper Pond with it shortly thereafter. Also to be considered is that, as the driver of the stolen Buick, Whitley would have been in the better position to have made the heart shot.

Nevertheless, Whitley maintained the story line that it was Taylor who had pulled the trigger on the bullet that killed the

Indiana trooper. He hoped no evidence to the contrary would surface. To have confessed to it at the time would have likely gotten him the death penalty. Years would pass before he would admit to it in writing, an admission that seems to have gone unnoticed.

VICTOR WHITLEY AT SEYMOUR POLICE BARRACKS
After Telling His Story, He Was Led Out For Arraignment

Compliments of the Indianapolis Star

PART C – AFTERMATH

"This is my shield, I bear it before me in battle,
But it is not mine alone.
It protects my brother on my left. It protects my city.
I will never let my brother out of its shadow,
Nor my city out of its shelter.
I will die with my shield before me,
Facing the enemy."
~ Steven Pressfield ~

Chapter XIV – FUNERALS

Hutch and Dug had shared a brotherhood as partners in the Michigan State Police. It is a special relationship born to those who have faced crises together. Not realizing it at the time, Hutch had shared Dug's last shift of patrol during the evening of September 29, 1957. Never to be forgotten was the promise he had made.

Trooper Warren Hutchinson would have never dreamed that three days later he would be the MSP escort for the hearse that transported Trooper Dugald Pellot's body from Tecumseh to his hometown of Lansing for the funeral. If it had to be, he was honored to be the one doing it. The next day, he would serve as one of six selected by Kay to serve as a pallbearer. That too would be a sad honor.

Kay had married at age 19, became a mother at 20, and was now a widow at 21. Her time between getting the life-changing news on the afternoon of September 30 to the funeral on October 3 was a blur.

During that blur, caring for their infant son provided some solace. In those precious moments of oneness, she vowed to herself to make certain that Greg would vicariously come to know his father.

Alice too was 19 years old, only a year out of high school, when she married Bill Kellems. For better or worse, she had no children to demand her attention. Like Pellot, Trooper William Kellems' body would also be escorted to his hometown for burial. It just so happened that both hometowns were their respective state capitals.

And so it was arranged: the troopers' funerals, with military honors, would occur on the same day, at the same time, in each state's capital city. The Indiana State Police would send a color guard squad to the Michigan funeral, which the Michigan State Police would do in kind. Officers from police departments across the country would join in the two processions to show their respect.

Far apart, each widow would witness the flag that had draped her husband's casket being folded with military crispness. And, as if a souvenir, the flag was then presented to her.

Absent from the funerals would be the hospitalized colleagues who suffered near miss heart shots while standing in harm's way: MSP Trooper Doug Vogel remained in an Ann Arbor hospital, ISP Trooper Bob Pond in an Indianapolis Hospital, and NVPD Patrolman Lester Kenens at the Seymour Hospital.

At age 23, Trooper Dugald A. Pellot became the 21st officer of the Michigan State Police to die in the line of duty since its establishment in 1917. On his tombstone is engraved, "In Valor there is Hope."

MSP Trooper Dugald A. Pellot

At age 27, Trooper William R. Kellems became the 13th officer of the Indiana State Police to die in the line of duty since its establishment in 1933. On the Indiana State Police Memorial, where his name is engraved with those of similar fate, are the words, "As we that are left behind grow old, they shall not grow old. Age shall not weary them nor the years condemn. At the going down of the sun and in the morning, WE SHALL REMEMBER THEM."

ISP Trooper William R. Kellems

Ralph Taylor's parents, sister, and estranged wife were contacted, but no one wanted his body. He would receive a pauper's burial in an unmarked grave, the county being reimbursed of the expense from the cash found in Taylor's billfold.

Ironically, the plot would be nearly within a stone's throw of where he had bounced down the road dead, having fallen from the fleeing police car.

At the burial there were witnesses, but no mourners. Victor Whitley was in jail.

One of the witnesses was young mortician Jerry Sharp from the Dowd Funeral Home. Fate had bestowed on him the solemn duty of collecting the body of Ralph Taylor from the side of the highway, preparing it for burial, and now witnessing it being planted in the ground. Never before had he provided these services for such an evil man. He hoped he never would again. Little did he know that in the years to come, he would be providing such services for many of the good men who had stood in harm's way on that day.

As the clumps of dirt fell on the vault, another witness to the burial, a North Vernon patrolman, muttered, "There would be two of them being buried today if that other guy [Whitley] had come out of the woods near me."

> *"Justice rarely satisfies all parties."*
> ~ Clif Edwards ~

Chapter XV – JUSTICE

Kenens' well-placed shot had served two purposes. It had saved the taxpayers a lot of money, and it had fulfilled Ralph Taylor's wish: he would not be going back to prison. Victor Whitley would be another matter.

In just ten hours, multiple heinous crimes, legally referred to as capital offenses, had been committed in two states. Where to initiate prosecution was obvious. Indiana had both Victor Whitley and the death penalty. Michigan had neither.

The day after being a party to shooting up two states, Whitley was arraigned before Justice of the Peace O. E. Hedrick and was bound over to the Scott County grand jury. He would be held without bond on the charge of murder.

Back then, Indiana initiated prosecution for cases of this nature through a grand jury. In that process, the prosecutor presents evidence to a randomly selected panel of citizens who decide whether to indict the defendant or not.

In this case, there would be two grand juries. One would be seated in Scott County to hear evidence about the murder of Trooper Kellems. Another would be seated in Jennings County for the shooting of Trooper Pond and Patrolman Kenens and for the kidnapping of Deputy Perkins.

A grand jury hears no defense to the charges sought and the hearings are secret. A grand jury can demand certain inquiries to be made and the outcomes reported to them. Harry E. McCalla acted as prosecutor in presenting the cases to the grand jury for each Indiana county.

For example, in this case the grand jury had a request concerning the woman's blood-soaked jacket found in the Buick, the car that had been stolen in Michigan and recovered in Indiana. They asked that it be shown to the once-kidnapped woman to see if she could identify it. ISP detectives flew to Michigan where they met with MSP detectives who arranged for Dorothea LeCronier to see the jacket. She identified it as hers.

After three days of deliberation, on Monday, October 6, 1957, the Scott County grand jury returned a first-degree murder indictment for Victor Whitley. One should know that it is a rule of law that accessories to the crime of murder can be charged the same as principals.

Whitley was retrieved from the Clark County jail in Jeffersonville to be formally charged in the courthouse in Scottsburg. Up until then he had been held in the Clark County jail as the Scott County jail was not considered secure enough for a person facing such serious charges. There he met his court-appointed attorney, Eugene Hough, who would represent Whitley on the Scott County charges. No one could have imagined how this relationship would pay dividends decades down the road.

From the arraignment in Scott County, Sheriff Charles Dudley transported Whitley to the Jennings County jail where he would await proceedings. As Dudley crossed the bridge where the shootout had occurred, he watched Whitley in his rearview mirror. Dudley later said, "We crossed the bridge where the gun battle took place, but if he [Whitley] recognized it, he didn't let on."

Now that Whitley was lodged in the Jennings County Jail, he and Deputy Clyde Perkins traded roles from their first meeting. Whitley was now Perkins' prisoner. Under the care and custody of Perkins, their relationship seemed to gradually change from antagonist to sympathizer. Whitley undoubtedly recognized that he needed a friend on the side that sought to punish and possibly execute him. Perhaps, once again, Whitley was exercising his gift of influence.

And while he waited in jail, the press, as they often do with notorious criminals, seemed to take an empathetic view of Victor Whitley. That was something he probably favored and fueled by granting interviews.

One paper reported him as remaining quiet in his cell, saying little and not in the best of spirits. They also wrote that he received quite a bit of mail from his ex-wife, mother, and grandmother. Also, he had a Bible.

Victor Whitley in jail

Picture from TRUE DETECTIVE – Jan 1958

When another reporter asked if he ever considered leaving Taylor, Whitley said, "I would have to leave the country if I did, and I couldn't do that."

The reporter responded, "You mean you thought he would kill you?"

Whitley answered, "I didn't think; I knew he would." He went on to describe Taylor as an overbearing man who often told him he was ready to die. In closing, Whitley said, "Ralph was just a no-good, I reckon."

Detroit Free Press reporter Carter Van Lopik described Whitley as "tall, blonde and well built, handsome in a way which would make many consider him a typical American boy – in looks, at least."

Referencing the son of fallen Michigan Trooper Dugald Pellot, Van Lopik quoted Whitley as saying, "From the little boy's standpoint a man like that [Taylor] doesn't have any business living." Whitley later added, "If somebody killed my wife, I'd do my best to get'em capital punishment."

In saying such things, Whitley pushed blame to his dead partner. In some circles, including one of his past hostages, sympathy grew.

On Monday, October 21, 1957, three weeks after the day of terror, the Jennings County grand jury indicted Victor Whitley on charges of kidnapping Deputy Clyde Perkins and the attempted murder of Trooper Robert Pond and Patrolman Lester Kenens. Bond was set at $5000 on each charge. With no bond on the murder charges in Scott County, it was a moot point; Whitley would remain in custody.

About six weeks after the shootings, on Thursday, November 14, 1957, Dudley, Perkins, and North Vernon Police Chief Rice transported Whitley from the Jennings County jail to court. Rumors suggested a deal had been struck between the defense and prosecution.

Apparently it was true, Whitley pled guilty to kidnapping Deputy Perkins, the strongest case, and the two attempted murder charges were dismissed. Following his plea, Judge Fred Matthews told him his sentence could include the electric chair.

The prosecutor made a motion that the judge delay sentencing until Whitley had been tried in Scott County on the murder charge. Whitley's pauper attorney in Jennings County was Ira Hamilton who argued against the motion. Denying the prosecutor's motion, the judge immediately sentenced Whitley to life in prison. Most folks did not realize that the sentence could, with good behavior, allow for parole after 17 years of imprisonment.

In letters to relatives, Whitley had written that he expected the death sentence. In court, Whitley stood stalwart, his trademark, and when sentenced he displayed no emotion. But, while being returned to jail, he was heard to emotionally utter to himself, "Somebody up there is still with me."

The next day, November 15, 1957, one year to the day after William Kellems had been appointed as a trooper in the Indiana State Police, Jennings County Sheriff Charles Dudley delivered Whitley to the Indiana Penitentiary in Michigan City, Indiana. There he would begin a prison sentence of life while awaiting trial for his part in the murder of Trooper Kellems.

During that waiting period, concerns arose that with the conviction and life sentence in Jennings County, the murder charge in Scott County might be dismissed.

Learning of the rumblings, ISP Major Paul T. Beverforden, who had paraded Whitley before the troopers who had hunted him, was quoted on November 1, 1957, in the Seymour Daily Tribune newspaper, saying, "This criminal should be dealt with to the full extent of the law. He should not be permitted to escape trial for murder. I have one of my boys dead. He was shot down in cold blood. I feel very strongly about that. The killer should answer for that crime. We are sure we can convict him."

Judge Fred S. Matthews, who had sentenced Whitley in Jennings County, was also the circuit court judge for Scott County. The prosecution moved for a change of judge. As a result, Judge Paul J. Tegart of Floyd County was appointed to hear the case.

Apparently, at least initially, the defense did not favor Tegart, so they took their turn in making a motion for another change of judge.

In response, Judge Tegart named a panel of three judges for the defense and prosecution to haggle over. The process provided that each side could dismiss one judge. The remaining one would then hear the case.

On March 25, 1958, almost six months after the day of terror and with the authorization of the governor, Whitley was transported back to the Jennings County jail to await hearings and trial in Scott County. Once again, he was held in the Jennings County jail as the Scott County jail was still not considered secure enough for such a criminal.

There, Whitley undoubtedly consulted with his attorney, Eugene Hough, about the upcoming hearing on judge selection and the case as a whole. Two days later, on March 27, 1958, in the Scott County circuit court with the family of fallen Trooper Kellems present, Whitley made a surprise move.

At the onset of the scheduled hearing, Whitley's attorney withdrew his motion for a change of judge, and Whitley pled guilty to the murder of Trooper Kellems. Absent a presentence investigation or hearing victims' statements, Judge Paul J. Tegart immediately sentenced him to life in prison, sparing him the electric chair.

Such an abrupt about face in Whitley's defense strategy and the immediate sentencing suggests some type of agreement had been made off the record, perhaps with a wink and nod. To have pled guilty to murder, the defense must have known it would save Whitley from a death sentence.

It is not known if the prosecution was complicit in the agreement. To that end, it did save the court from the expense of a trial and saved the prosecution from the risk of a not guilty verdict, a risk every trial brings.

And with his life saved, Whitley eloquently said to the court, "I thank the people of Indiana for their mercy." A most polished remark, it refutes the notion that it was spontaneous.

Present for the surprise move was Alice, Trooper Kellems' widow, and his brother and parents. When it was over, his brother said, "I'm glad it is closed. There is nothing the court could do to bring the trooper back."

And with the ringing of the gavel to close the case, Whitley was whisked back to the penitentiary.

Since you can only serve one life sentence, it would have to be concurrent to the same sentence he was serving for his guilty plea in Jennings County. On one hand the penalty appeared as nothing. On the other it was some insurance as this life sentence did not have the option of parole. Also, in the event one conviction was later overturned, the other would stand.

Most law enforcement was disappointed there was no death penalty, but there was some consolation that he would die in prison. Or so they believed.

Surrounding these court proceedings, Whitley was mostly held in the Jennings County Jail, again often under the watchful eye of Deputy Sheriff Clyde Perkins, the officer he had kidnapped at gunpoint on that nightmarish night. During this time, it appears their relationship continued to develop. In the years to come, it would appear that Perkins not only forgave Whitley, but came to view him as one of Taylor's many victims.

One can only wonder what influence Perkins may have had on Whitley being spared the death sentence twice. And, as if that weren't enough, there would be dividends that would be paid in the future.

Meanwhile, MSP investigated the Michigan crimes in the event Indiana failed in serving justice. Before Taylor was buried, Sergeant Fred O'Donnell was flown down and viewed his body, identifying him as the person who had killed Trooper Dugald Pellot. In viewing the crease O'Donnell's bullet likely put in Taylor's skull, he undoubtedly wished, like no other bullet he had ever fired, that this one would have been a bullseye.

Like Indiana, Michigan had capital offenses committed in two different counties: Lenawee and Jackson. Unlike Indiana, Michigan seldom used a grand jury. A Michigan prosecutor primarily adhered to the complaint warrant system. The decision to authorize a complaint warrant fell to the prosecutor and a judge who would have to be convinced by a sworn complainant that probable cause existed before issuing the warrant.

As cases go, Chief Assistant Jackson County Prosecutor George Beach had a pretty clear-cut one. He only needed detectives to complete a few things before he authorized the complaint for a warrant.

On October 16, 1957, the 36-year-old kidnap victim, Dorothea LeCronier, was flown to Indiana to view a corporeal line-up at the Jennings County jail. Before her stood five white men, all of similar appearance. Between her and the five men was a row of bars. Standing behind stage lights pointed at the row of men, she could see them well. It was quite the opposite for them.

She was then asked if she recognized any of them. In an emotional voice, she pointed to the fourth man, Victor Whitley, and said, "Yes." She went on to say that he was one of the two men who had posed as FBI agents, bound her in a jackknife position in the back seat of a Studebaker, and then had stolen her car.

After the line-up, she was taken to where her red-and-white Buick was stored. There she made her second identification of the day, although her car was now shot full of bullet holes.

126

On November 6, 1957, a warrant was issued out of Jackson County, Michigan, against Victor Whitley for kidnapping Dorothea LeCronier.

In Lenawee County, Trooper Vogel had been wounded, Trooper Pellot murdered, and Citizen Crowe kidnapped and his car stolen. In both shootings, there were witnesses that established Taylor as the shooter. Whitley was not even present when Pellot was murdered.

Detectives searched for evidence of a conspiracy between Taylor and Whitley to commit murder, but it was unfruitful. They also pursued a theory of felony murder with the elements being that Whitley was a party to a felony which was the catalyst to a murder. They submitted their completed investigation to the Lenawee County prosecutor and awaited his decision.

Undoubtedly many sleepless nights would pass before Prosecutor Kenneth Glaser responded in a heartfelt 4-page letter addressed to Sergeant O'Donnell, dated November 6, 1957. In it the prosecutor articulated in legal detail the reasons he did not feel it would be proper jurisprudence to charge Whitley with the shooting of Vogel and murder of Pellot.

On page 3 of his letter, Prosecutor Glaser wrote "that such warrants issued against Victor Whitley would not be supported by the law and facts presently in our possession. We might possibly find a very slim basis for same by saying that Whitley and Taylor had a general purpose to commit armed robbery wherever they had the opportunity. However, Whitley states that they had no intention of doing so in this state, but were going to trade a car in Detroit, and we have no evidence to the contrary. My opinion is that this theory would not stand up in court, and I have found nothing that I felt supported such a theory under the known facts of our case."

In consolation, on November 27, 1957, Glaser authorized a two-count warrant for the armed robbery and kidnapping of Henry Crowe. Off the record, with Crowe being 72 years of age, the prosecutor expressed concern about how many years he would be available as a witness.

With a kidnapping warrant out of Jackson County and a two-count warrant for kidnapping and armed robbery out of Lenawee County, Michigan stood ready to pick up the ball should Indiana fumble. The kidnapping charges were a capital offense carrying a life sentence.

To that end, MSP detectives then sent certified copies of the warrants to the Indiana State Penitentiary in Michigan City, Indiana, to be placed as a detainer in the event that Whitley would ever be released or paroled. If that occurred, Indiana was supposed to notify Michigan so that Michigan could then extradite him to stand trial.

With that completed, MSP detectives sent their evidence and reports to long-term storage, making it available if ever needed. They then went on to other cases.

Nearly six months had passed since the terror of September 30, 1957, when Whitley was returned to the Indiana prison, now with a second life sentence. That seemed to seal his fate. It was believed that Whitley would never again be a free man, even without considering the capital offense charges being held in abeyance in Michigan. One might call it a failsafe.

"Perseverance is more prevailing than violence; and many things which cannot be overcome when they are together, yield themselves up when taken little by little."
~ Plutarch~

Chapter XVI – FORGIVEN

In his quasi-trance, Whitley had once again lived the events that had landed him in prison when, while still standing at parade-rest, he heard the distinctive shuffle of the courier approaching. He was jolted alert when he heard his prison nickname, "Hey Tex, I got something for you." Like a robot, Whitley stuck his hand through the bars, revealing his bullet-scarred thumb from some twenty years ago.

Envelope in hand, he withdrew to his bunk where he sat. The letter was from the "Office of the Indiana State Public Defender." It was what he had been impatiently waiting for. He wondered if its contents would continue the impasse, or if he might finally be granted a clemency hearing. For years it had been a futile effort.

Whittler would have been another fitting nickname for Whitley. Looking back, his whittling away of penalties had begun in Jennings County on November 14, 1957, when he pled guilty to kidnapping Deputy Clyde Perkins in exchange for dismissal of the charges of attempting to murder Trooper Robert Pond and Patrolman Lester Kenens. For that, he escaped the death penalty and was sentenced to life in prison.

In Scott County on March 27, 1958, he again dodged the death sentence when at the advice of his attorney, Eugene Hough, he pled guilty to the murder of Trooper William Kellems. Once more he was sentenced to life in prison, which was kind of a joke because he only had one life to live.

Prison mandates patience. The 1960s was a decade of doing his time while being a model inmate. And with its passage, he could only hope that public sentiment would fade with the passing of victims. Even more than he could have possibly hoped for was that his once attorney, Eugene Hough, had become the Scott County Circuit Judge in 1967.

In the early 1970s, with the assistance of the public defender's office, Whitley began to file for legal relief. His first petition for clemency was filed in Jennings County, dated June 15, 1972. Within it there is a revealing sentence. Difficult to see in the below excerpt from the court file, it reads, "During the confrontations, I kidnapped one officer and took the life of one officer." It would seem that after saying for all those years that it was Taylor that shot Trooper Kellems, he was now admitting to it. His motion was denied.

Following is a brief statement of circumstances surrounding the crime:

A series of robberies started in May, 1957, and ended in September, 1957, with a confrontation with various law enforcement agencies. During the confrontation, I kidnapped one officer and took the life of one officer.

Names of Co-defendants:

Clemency is asked for the following reasons:

During these 14 years of incarceration, I have developed a self-discipline, an emotional control, and a sense of responsibility that I sorely lacked at the time of my criminal activities—a period of 5 months, from May to September, 1957. I honestly believe that I can return to society with a respectful and healthy attitude toward its members.

The next year, Whitley would begin to file petitions for clemency in Scott County where he had pled guilty to murder. He would do so in April of 1973, 1975, 1976, 1977, and 1978. All of these motions were denied.

Finally, another star aligned for Whitley. In 1980, with Judge Hough in his final year of judgeship, Clyde Perkins once more entered the picture. Perkins, the deputy Whitley had once kidnapped and who had subsequently become sympathetic to him, became the judge's bailiff. In that position, Perkins would have the ear of Judge Hough.

In light of that, after so many failed attempts, Whitley again applied for a clemency hearing. The letter the courier had just delivered would tell him the outcome.

Sitting on his bunk, he carefully unsealed the envelope. Methodically he withdrew its contents, a twice-folded piece of paper. Now in his mid-forties, he squinted as he read. As he did, a smile began to form.

Finally, Judge Eugene Hough had granted him a clemency hearing, to be heard on June 13, 1980. Having previously been Whitley's attorney, Hough had to recuse himself from the hearing. In doing so, he appointed retired Judge Tegart, the same judge who had sentenced Whitley to life in prison in 1958, to adjudicate it.

At the clemency hearing, Judge Eugene Hough, Bailiff Clyde Perkins, and Defendant Victor Whitley testified. Clyde Perkins' testimony would be different from the statements he had made immediately following the incident. Some twenty-plus years later, Perkins would testify he never saw Whitley hold a gun, which contradicted a statement he made to an ISP detective shortly after the incident.

When Perkins was done testifying at the clemency hearing, he was asked by Judge Tegart, "Are you in favor of the court granting relief to Whitley?"

Perkins answered, "I am."

Whitley then took the stand, and through his attorney painted a picture that made him appear a victim rather than a villain. Whitley expressed that he had been totally dominated by the notorious Ralph Taylor and that Taylor had actually done the shootings. He said, "Everything that occurred in that four-month period was contrary to my nature. It was just the opposite of the way I was raised."

When the hearing was complete, Judge Tegart granted Whitley clemency, reducing the murder conviction to "Accessory after the fact of Manslaughter." He then resentenced him to 2-21 years in prison with credit for time served. Judge Tegart said what had swayed him the most was the testimony of Clyde Perkins.

With that ruling, Whitley was absolved of continued imprisonment out of Scott County and he became eligible for parole on the still-standing Jennings County conviction for kidnapping. His parole hearing was scheduled for December 3, 1980, and he was told that he would be the only person allowed to speak. All others would have to submit a signed letter expressing their views.

Alice Kellems, the widow of Trooper William R. Kellems, opposed parole and submitted this letter saying so:

CONFIDENTIAL

December 2, 1980

Recvd 12-2-80 A.T.

Mr. Albert P. Tutsie, Chairman
Indiana Parole Board
803 State Office Building
100 North Senate Avenue
Indianapolis, Indiana 46204

Attention: Glenn E. Douthitt, Member

Dear Mr. Tutsie:

I understand that VICTOR WAYNE WHITLEY will be considered for parole tomorrow, December 3, 1980, due to some sort of court action.

I feel that I, as the widow of slain Trooper William R. Kellems, have the right to voice an opinion and I would like to make this my official request that this parole not be granted.

As in the past, I have strongly objected to his clemency, parole or release, along with his parents, brothers and sister and other relatives, and the Indiana State Police. I feel it would be a great injustice for his release.

Thank you for taking the time to consider my request.

Sincerely,

Mrs. William R. Kellems

RESTRICTED

This is a true and accurate copy of a document on file with the Indiana State Archives
Ind. Archives and Records Admin.
6440 E. 30th Street
Indianapolis, IN 46219

From Indiana Archives & Records

No surprise, John Shettle, the superintendent of the Indiana State Police, also expressed his opposition to parole in this letter:

HEADQUARTERS
INDIANA STATE POLICE
INDIANAPOLIS

CONFIDENTIAL

OFFICE OF THE SUPERINTENDENT

December 1, 1980

INDIANA PAROLE BOARD
RECEIVED
DEC 1 1980
RECEIVED
CLEMENCY COMMISSION

TO: Albert P. Tutsie, Chairman
          Parole Board
          Department of Corrections

FROM: John T. Shettle, Superintendent
          Indiana State Police Department

SUBJECT: Parole Hearing - Victor W. Whitley
          ISP #29646

Mr. Whitley is currently serving a life sentence for the kidnapping for ransom of Deputy Sheriff Clyde Perkins.

He was also committed to life imprisonment for the first degree murder of Trooper William Kellems. This sentence has recently been reduced, making him eligible for parole. He is appearing for a parole hearing on Wednesday, December 3, 1980.

The nature of these extremely serious crimes committed against law enforcement officers as they were performing their duties must be the deciding factors in your deliberations.

On behalf of the Indiana State Police Department, I enter an objection and request that you deny his petition.

John T. Shettle
John T. Shettle
Superintendent

RESTRICTED

JTS:bb

From Indiana Archives & Records

Since the parole hearing concerned the kidnapping conviction in which Clyde Perkins was the victim, one wonders if he communicated to the parole board his feelings concerning it. If so, no record of this was found.

When the parole hearing ended, Whitley likely wondered how he had represented himself. It was a good sign when two weeks later, he was transferred to the Westville Work Release Center where he would be observed while living in a pre-parole lifestyle.

In that transition, he would share a two-bedroom duplex with another and work as a laborer doing prison grounds maintenance, earning $3.35 an hour. Whitley undoubtedly knew he had six months to prove himself, and he was committed to doing so.

When June of 1981 came, Whitley became increasingly anxious to get his mail as he knew any day his parole ruling would arrive. It was undoubtedly a similar feeling to what Trooper Kellems would have felt, had he lived to wait to learn if he would be advanced to Trooper First Class.

Whitley did not have to wait long. On Wednesday, June 3, 1981, when he came home from work, he again checked his mailbox. There a letter waited from the parole board. He carefully grasped it and then walked to the privacy of his bedroom to read its contents.

At age 49, Victor Whitley was granted parole. Perhaps, just as when sentenced in Jennings County so long ago, he again looked up and said, "Somebody up there is still with me." Ironically, being experienced and having proved himself as a good employee, he was then hired at full wage to work for the Indiana prison system.

Three years later, on January 3, 1984, he was released from parole. Victor Whitley was now truly a free man. He would continue to work for the state until he retired in 1996. During those years he married Laverne (Perrine) Whitley and acquired stepchildren. He also acquired a nice country home on a bluff that provided him a splendid view of sunsets, something he had dearly missed during his years in prison.

Having paid his debt to Indiana, Whitley probably wondered if Michigan officials would now appear and demand their due for the kidnappings he had done there so long ago.

It was early 2013 when MSP Detective Sergeant Michael Knauf received a tip that the surviving suspect in the shooting of Trooper Douglas Vogel and murder of Trooper Dugald Pellot had been released from an Indiana prison.

Knowing little of the 1957 incident, which had occurred before he was born but happened in the district he was now assigned, Knauf began to research the incident. Fitting the half-century-old case into more current matters would make it a slow process.

Buried in the records division at headquarters is where he would find the lengthy report. In the long-term storage facility, he located the evidence. Bit by bit, as time permitted, he reviewed his findings.

According to the faded reports, detainers had been filed with the Indiana prison system advising them to notify the MSP should Whitley ever be released so they could then initiate extradition to Michigan for prosecution. It had now been 32 years since Whitley had been paroled, and he found no record that notification had ever taken place.

It would appear that with the passing of time, the Michigan detainers for Victor Whitley had been lost. Or, possibly, a previous MSP detective had failed to document a "nolle prosequi" decision made years earlier and close the inactive file.

Through the course of the reactivated investigation, Knauf consulted the relevant Michigan prosecutors. With the Michigan kidnap victims now dead, he was told that prosecution was no longer an option and to close the dormant case.

The case would be transferred to Detective Sergeant Larry Rothman for closure. On September 11, 2017, Rothman telephoned Victor Whitley. He told him that the Michigan cases were being closed, which meant he need not worry about being prosecuted for them.

In closing, Rothman asked Whitley if there was anything he would like to say after all those years. Whitley said he could not begin to say how sorry he was for what had happened.

Perhaps "failsafe," the last word at the end of Chapter 15 – Justice, should have been "guarantee." In Michigan, the statute of limitations for the crime of kidnapping is ten years. Kidnapping was the most serious charge in the warrants issued in Michigan. In this case, the ten-year guarantee would have expired on September 30, 1967.

It could be argued that the statute of limitations would have been tolled with Whitley being out of state. The counter-argument could be that Michigan knew where Whitley was in Indiana and could have extradited him to stand trial. Not doing so, arguments for Whitley might include violations of the right to due process and a speedy trial. A judge would have had to decide.

For those ten years, had for some reason the convictions in Indiana been overturned, Michigan was well poised to step in, at least in Jackson County, and extradite Whitley to Michigan to stand trial. Dorothea LeCronier, who had been kidnapped in Jackson County, did not die until May 2017.

Harry Crowe, the first person the duo kidnapped on that fateful day, died in September 1964, ending the likelihood of a successful prosecution in Lenawee County.

Those touched by the terror of that day might argue that Whitley should have been extradited back to Michigan during that ten year time period to stand trial for the kidnappings. At the time Whitley was serving two life sentences in Indiana, one without a parole option.

Had Whitley been convicted in Michigan, he could have been given a third and fourth life sentence. However, it is very probable the prison time would be served concurrently, and furthermore those sentences would have a parole option.

So, even if Whitley had been tried and convicted in Michigan with life sentences, it is likely he would have been paroled in 1981.

Justice seldom satisfies all parties.

> *"What we leave behind in our lives*
> *may help someone else find the way."*
> ~ Author Unknown ~

Chapter XVII – SURVIVORS

By all accounts, MSP Trooper Dugald Pellot and ISP Trooper William Kellems died quickly while doing what they felt born to do. They had been cheated of their rightful time, but there was likely little pain in their passing.

One is reminded of the poem by Laurence Binyon:

> *They went with songs to the battle, they were young*
> *Straight of limb, true of eye, steady and aglow.*
> *They were staunch to the end against odds uncounted*
> *They fell with their faces to the foe.*
>
> *They shall not grow old, as we that are left grow old.*
> *Age shall not weary them, nor the years condemn.*
> *At the going down of the sun and in the morning*
> *We will remember them.*

The first verse speaks to the fallen. The second to the survivors, left behind to cope with the aftermath of that tragic day.

Jennings County (IN) Sheriff Charles Dudley had miraculously avoided injury on that day. At the time he was in his second term as sheriff. For his courage, the Indiana Sheriff Association named him Sheriff of the Year. As his term neared its end, he resigned to campaign to be elected county auditor. This made his deputy, Clyde Perkins, the sheriff to finish the term and positioned Perkins well for the next election.

Unfortunately for Dudley, the voters did not elect him to be the county auditor. He later became the director of security for the Muscatatuck State Hospital.

At age 64, with failing health, Charles Dudley took his own life on December 11, 1974. ISP Lieutenant Robert Pond, who had once stood by Dudley in a perilous gun battle and who was now the commander of the Seymour Post, assigned Trooper Charles Waggoner to investigate Dudley's death. It was determined to be a suicide.

Charles Dudley is remembered as a most effective sheriff, soft-spoken, considerate, gentle but firm, and calm in crisis. Of the good and evil that collided on that day, Dudley would be the second to be serviced by the Dowd-Dove Funeral Home.

MSP Sergeant Frederick O'Donnell, the second officer to engage Ralph Taylor in a gunfight, would receive a bravery award for his part in the events of September 30, 1957. In that shootout, it is believed that one of the bullets he fired creased the head of Ralph Taylor.

O'Donnell would later be promoted to lieutenant and transferred to Fifth District Headquarters in Paw Paw where he would serve out his MSP career. On March 7, 1977, he died of cancer.

North Vernon (IN) Patrolman Lester (Tiny) Kenens, who is credited with shooting Ralph Taylor dead, came home from the Hospital some ten days later. Several of those days, he had lain in a coma, while his wife and five children worried about the outcome. Next to his heart remained Whitley's bullet, which doctors felt was too risky to remove.

It would take three months of recuperation before Kenens would be able to return to work. Forevermore, he would be hampered by the now crippled third finger on his right hand, which had also been shot by Whitley. His son often heard him say, "I wish they would have cut it off." For his brave acts on that fateful day, he was named North Vernon Officer of the Year.

Kenens served 7½ years with the North Vernon police, rising to the rank of captain. In 1962, he opposed Clyde Perkins as the Democratic nominee for Jennings County Sheriff and lost. Apparently with no hard feelings and with mutual respect, Kenens then worked for Perkins as a deputy sheriff.

Deputy Sheriff Lester (Tiny) Kenens

Compliments of Michael Kenens, son of Lester Kenens

Kenens also became a firefighter, did some farming, and owned and operated Tiny's Fire Extinguisher Service. He was considered by many as a pioneer in being a school resource officer. He was certainly a hero on September 30, 1957.

Years after the shootout, a boil appeared on Kenens' shoulder. When a doctor treated it, he discovered the cause. The bullet that Whitley had planted in him years earlier had finally worked itself to the surface. Kenens' son, Mike, had a tie-tack made from it.

In early 1979, Kenens suffered a heart attack. When the doctor examined him, he discovered Kenens to have a damaged heart and presumed that he had experienced a previous heart attack. The doctor later concluded that the damage had been caused when he was heart shot by Whitley.

Following that heart attack, on February 14, 1979, Kenens died at age 60. He would be the third to be serviced by the Dowd-Dove Funeral Home, the same place that had handled the funeral of the man he had killed many years earlier.

Jennings County (IN) Deputy Sheriff Clyde Perkins, who had been kidnapped by Victor Whitley, would follow Charles Dudley in being sheriff. He served in that capacity from 1959 to 1968. It would appear he then took a sabbatical from public service, being a heating and air conditioning contractor. He then served as the circuit court bailiff for Jennings and Scott County from 1980 to 1986. Bailiffs are often close friends with the judge for whom they serve. It would appear that this relationship was of significant benefit to Whitley.

On June 26, 1988, at age 77, Clyde Perkins died. Like three of the men he endured combat with on September 30, 1957, Charles Dudley, Lester Kenens, and Ralph Taylor, he would be the fourth serviced by Jerry Sharp, now part owner of the Dove-Sharp Funeral Home.

No matter how one feels about Perkins being a character witness for Whitley, one has to applaud his courage to do what he thought was right.

ISP Trooper Robert Pond, a week after being shot in the hand by Whitley, returned home wearing a cast. Doctors felt that in time he would be able to return to duty, and he did. For his actions, he was awarded the Indiana State Police Valor Award, symbolized by a gold star.

Pond served with the ISP from 1955 to 1979, rising to the rank of lieutenant and becoming the District Commander out of the Seymour Post. His troopers remember him as a fair commander who always seemed to know what was important and what wasn't. He seldom spoke about the gold star worn on his uniform. After ISP retirement, he worked as a Jennings County probation officer. On June 27, 2000, at age 72, Robert Pond died.

Alice and ISP Trooper William Kellems had been married 5 years when he was murdered. Following it, she chose to fulfill her husband's mission to serve the Indiana State Police, doing so as a civilian employee. During her 43 years of service, she rose to the position of "Head Personnel and Training Secretary," retiring in 2000.

In 2007, at age 74, Alice died. She was buried beside her fallen trooper. She asked that contributions be made to the widows of the Indiana State Police.

Kay, the widow of MSP Trooper Dugald Pellot, kept her promise, making sure that their son, Greg, came to know his father vicariously. It was through the generosity of the Hundred Club of Detroit paying his tuition that Greg was able to attend Michigan State University. He graduated with a degree in marketing and electrical engineering and lives the life of a fine citizen. And in doing so, he gives back in many ways, to include being a guardian for veterans on Honor Flights to Washington, D.C. His father's name, Dugald, has been passed on to his male descendants.

Kay eventually remarried. She made her way in life as a mother, model, actress, and she is an advocate of TBL (Thin Blue Line) and COPS (Concerns of Police Survivors). Engraved on her fallen trooper's gravestone are two names, Trooper Dugald Pellot and hers. One day she will again lie at his side.

Warren Hutchinson, Pellot's partner on his final patrol, also kept his promise, staying in touch to make sure Kay and Greg were doing okay.

When MSP Trooper Douglas Vogel was released from the hospital, his wife, Marilyn, and post commander, Sergeant Fred O'Donnell, were waiting to take him home.

Marilyn and Doug Vogel with Sergeant O'Donnell

Picture from Kay Pellot Andersen's scrapbook. Origin unknown

Vogel would return to light duty on November 18, and later to full duty. Easing back into patrol, it would be Trooper Warren Hutchinson, whom Vogel had once provided field training, that would take him out for his return to the road. After their first traffic stop, Hutchinson could tell that Vogel was visibly shaken. Gradually, his confidence appeared to return.

Vogel would be the third officer in the history of the Michigan State Police to be awarded the Valor Citation while still living. It was his intuition that had uncovered the criminal ways of Taylor and Whitley, leading to a shootout in which he was seriously wounded. A hero, with a wife and now five children, he would soon be promoted to detective and transferred to Detroit.

Since Vogel was the one who had sparked the tragic events, one wonders if he struggled with what has been called "survivor's guilt." At that time, Post Traumatic Stress Disorder (PTSD) was not recognized. His family would suffer from its symptoms when he became alcoholic and abusive. A divorce followed.

Eventually these symptoms affected his work, and under pressure he resigned from the MSP. Douglas Vogel would struggle with relationships and employment for the remainder of his life. He once told his son, "You don't know how it feels to have a man look you in the eye as he shoots you."

In the early 1980s, he learned that Victor Whitley had been released. He was advised that if Whitley ever tried to contact him to report it. In response, Vogel told his son, "If I ever see him, I'll kill him on the spot."

In November of 2003, at age 74, he died from respiratory failure at St. Joseph Hospital in Ann Arbor, Michigan. It was the same hospital that had treated him for his gunshot wounds some 45 years earlier.

145

In 2019, Robert Vogel, Trooper Douglas Vogel's only son, met with Gregory Pellot, Trooper Dugald Pellot's only son, both men in their sixties. Bob would say to Greg, "On September 30, 1957, you lost your dad, and I began to lose mine."

The back cover of this book begins with Ten hours, nine heroes . . . On that dreadful day, eight officers bravely stood in harm's way confronting the criminals. So, you may ask who was the ninth hero? Exercising author authority, I have nominated Nora Nichols, the only civilian and female to oppose Taylor and Whitley, and in doing so turned the tide of momentum.

Nora Nichols would return to Urbana, Ohio where she would live out her life raising her family. She passed in 2014.

And, so it would be: Victor Whitley would be the last combatant still standing from that dark day in the history of the Michigan and Indiana State Police.

This picture was taken at the Michigan State Police award ceremony. At it, Commissioner Joseph Childs presents Trooper Douglas Vogel (left) and Mrs. Dugald Pellot, on behalf of her fallen husband, the Valor award and Sergeant Frederick O'Donnell (right) the Bravery Award.

Compliments of Michael O'Donnell, son of Sergeant O'Donnell

Chapter XVIII– HAUNTED

Like silent sentries, the statues of lions guarded the entrances to the National Law Enforcement Memorial in Washington, D.C. As a retired officer, and now author of the *Paths Crossed* series, I felt drawn to this place. In the oppressive heat reflecting from the concrete, I entered reverently, seeking out the engraved names of colleagues I once knew, and others that I felt like I had known. As I did, I felt encircled by heroes that watched my every move.

In their memory, I posted pictures taken of their engraved names on my Facebook page. Soon after leaving, I got a ghostly message: "My husband's name is engraved there but I have not been there to see it." We began to message back and forth.

I learned the messenger was the widow of fallen Michigan Trooper Dugald Pellot, and that she had attended the MSP retiree banquet a month earlier. There she had won as a door prize a copy of my first book, *Paths Crossed: Villains-Victims-Victors,* which is about the Michigan State Police. Back and forth we messaged, sparking what would become an endearing friendship.

It would not be until the following January 2019 that our paths crossed. Over coffee and pastries, she showed me a remarkable scrapbook that she had created about the incident that had claimed her husband's life. At that moment, I recognized it as a shocking story that had waited over sixty years to be told. Researching and then writing a book about it became this author's next calling.

Having been a Michigan State Police Officer who had served in Lenawee and Jackson counties, I was familiar with the places where Taylor and Whitley had committed their Michigan crimes.

In my research, I would realize that the location where Taylor had shot Trooper Vogel was the same spot, where at age 13 while bicycling on now US-12, I witnessed an MSP patrol car do a power turn in front of me. It is odd the things we remember.

I also learned that of all the combatants of that fateful day, the only one still alive was Victor Whitley. I decided to contact him, hoping he would share his side of the story and provide insight into his deceased partner-in-crime.

On October 20, 2019, I telephoned him. My rings activated an outdated answering machine, and I listened to the tape recording of an old man's voice. I then left a message in which I identified myself as Clif Edwards, an author that was going to write a book about the events he was involved in on September 30, 1957. I explained that I wanted to give him an opportunity to tell his side of the story. I left my phone number and asked that he call me.

I then traveled to southern Indiana to gain as much first-hand knowledge of the Indiana side of the incident as possible. I visited the spot where Trooper William Kellems was shot dead, and then traveled the route that Whitley had driven from the murder to the shootouts at the bridge over the Muscatatuck River.

I then found and interviewed Melvin Ray, now an old man, who had once provided comfort to Trooper Kellems as he died. Next, I found and interviewed Jerry Sharp, the man who had collected the dead body of Ralph Taylor from the road, and then buried him three days later.

Victor Whitley did not return my phone call. During the late afternoon hours of October 23, 2019, I twice drove by Victor Whitley's home in southeast Indiana. I found it to be a pleasant-looking and well-kept two-story country home with a wrap-around porch. It sat on a bluff which would provide a view of the setting sun.

The large yard was mowed, but there was no car in the driveway. Perhaps, I thought, it was in the garage. With drapes drawn, the house appeared vacant. I wondered if he might be a snowbird and had already migrated south for the winter. When I drove by the second time, a deer grazed in his yard, the light of the setting sun reflecting off its tawny fur.

I waited until after dark before making my third and final drive by of the day. There was only one light on in the house. I thought it might be on a timer, meant to make it appear as if someone were home. I then went to a nearby Walmart parking lot. There I parked my camper van in a level spot, turned the engine off, and closed curtains so I could write in private.

Like so many times long ago, I was once again hidden in plain sight as I prepared for what might come should I find my quarry. This time it was an 88-year-old man.

Employing my rusty detective skills, I brainstormed themes intended to persuade him to talk. I jotted down fourteen questions to ask should I succeed. Feeling as prepared as I could be, I turned off the light and slept well.

Awake at first light, I boiled water on the stove of the van. From it, I prepared my strong, black, pour-through coffee. As I did, I also prepared breakfast. I measured a quarter cup of raw old-fashioned oats, a tablespoon of peanut butter powder, and a teaspoon of cinnamon into a bowl. Using the fork end of my spork, I mixed it. I then drenched it in steaming hot water. While it stewed, I sipped my coffee. Five minutes later, I sprinkled the concoction with walnuts and raisins and smothered it in yogurt. Now using the spoon end of the spork, I shoveled the tasty mush into my pie hole.

As I ate, I phoned a friend, a retired police officer, and told her my plan. I provided her the address of where I would be at 9:00 a.m. and the phone number for the police department for that area.

I requested that if I hadn't called her back by 9:30 a.m., that she call my cell phone. If I didn't answer, she should then call the police and ask that they go to that address to check on the welfare of a retired Michigan State Police officer, turned author, who had gone there to interview Victor Whitley, a man involved in the shooting of several Michigan and Indiana police officers in 1957.

As I ended the phone call, I wondered what my reaction would have been when I was a police officer, if I had been dispatched to such a call.

That morning I parked in the driveway marked by a mailbox labeled Victor Whitley. Nothing had changed since my drive-by the day before, except the deer was absent.

After much consideration, I decided to leave my pistol in the van. If it went bad, of the primal survival instincts of fight, flight, freeze, I hoped flight would allow me to get away. Wearing good running shoes, I walked onto the wooden porch. The window blinds were closed and again I thought the house was vacant. I knocked with purpose and then paused to listen. Nothing.

Again I knocked and listened. Around the corner of the wrap-around porch, out of sight, I heard something. Yes, someone was coming my way. I walked to meet whatever was making the sound.

At the corner, I met a neatly groomed and dressed, bespectacled old man. I introduced myself by name, and then turned and gazed to the west and said, "I bet you see great sunsets from here." When I turned back to him, I could see that my compliment had been well received. "Are you Victor Whitley?" I asked. He said he was.

I went on to explain that I was an author and that I was writing a book about September 30, 1957, and the events leading to and following it. Like in my previous message, I did not mention that I was a retired police officer.

I sensed I had poked a nerve. To me, Whitley seemed to be thinking: "Oh no, this might be the person I hoped would never come. I hope he won't finish what he is starting. I would rather the whole story be lost to time."

I then told him I would like to include his side of the incidents. He answered, "Why would I want to do that?" He was clearly competent.

I mentally selected my most fitting theme and countered with it. "When we reach our age, we start thinking about the legacy we leave behind. On September 30, 1957, you were involved in a lot of bad things. Perhaps your side of the story would not make you appear so evil."

He responded, "I've served my time. I've since retired from a good job. I have a family and they know who I am. That's all that matters."

Not ready to surrender theme one, I said, "Yesterday I met with the stepson of the late Clyde Perkins. You remember Clyde. You once kidnapped him and years later he testified on your behalf for clemency. His stepson told me that his dad always said good things about you. That is the side I would like to get to know and share in my book." My plea was greeted with silence.

I decided to change themes. "A couple of days ago, I spoke to the son of one of the Michigan troopers that was shot . . ."

Whitley interrupted me, "I didn't shoot any Michigan troopers."

I continued, "I know that, and you and I know the case in Michigan is closed and you need not fear any prosecution. But, that son of the Michigan trooper said that your sharing might bring peace and closure to a bitterness he has had for you his entire life."

Getting no response, I tried another theme, "Your partner, Ralph Taylor, I don't want to say he was a good bad guy; let's say he was a very trained bad guy. Do you know how he acquired those skills? Was he in the military?"

Whitley cut me off. "I don't know anything about that man."

"Progress," I thought, as I asked, "Is it true that the two of you first met when he picked you up hitchhiking in Maine?"

"It is," he answered.

Thinking I had opened him up, I paused to carefully frame my next question. Before I presented it, Whitley said, "It's time for you to go."

Hoping for a second chance, I said, "I respect that and will. Is it okay if I leave you a card? That way, if you later change your mind, you will be able to contact me."

"I don't want your card. Besides, I have your name and phone number from the message you left on my answering machine." His words and body language communicated impatience. Ignoring training and instincts, I turned my back to him and walked to my van.

As I drove away, I phoned my friend and told her that although I had failed in getting him to talk, I was safe and gone. She asked how I felt about it. "I have mixed emotions. On one hand, I do wish he would have shared his version of the story. On the other, if I were he, I would like to think I would not have talked either. Why would a person relive what was probably the worst day of their life?"

For a few minutes in time, some 62 years after that dark day in the history of the Michigan and Indiana State Police, Victor Whitley's and Clif Edwards' paths crossed. I was probably the person Victor Whitley hoped would never come knocking.

The return trip would take a two-day drive, making for a lot of alone time. Time to think. It had been just over ten months since this book had come knocking at my door. Over sixty years of waiting had exhausted its patience. Since conceived, the book had persistently haunted my subconscious. It required all my self-discipline not to stray from finishing *Battling Drug Dealers,* the book I had been writing for the past 18 months.

But sometimes I cheated. Like going to Indiana to do this research, justifying the trip because of circumstances and logistics.

During this trip, I had hoped to win the cooperation of Victor Whitley, and in doing so come to better understand the mental state of the murderous duo. I had failed.

Once again, I would have to revert to what detectives refer to as legwork. As a past cold case detective, legwork was something I had experience at. It would lead to many more paths crossed.

THE END

AFTERWORD

The "Good Old Days" were not always so good. A true story such as this reminds us that crime and violence have always been with us. What has been coined as the "thin blue line" keeps anarchy at bay. How many officers have fallen since the murder of Michigan Trooper Dugald Pellot and Indiana Trooper William Kellems? One could check, but the findings would not be accurate for very long. The list grows.

And as it does, in a democracy the citizens watch those who police and critique how this thin blue line is held. Different viewpoints see the same things differently and seek to change the rules of engagement. The author would suggest that when incidents are called into question, transparency is essential, and the secrecy of a grand jury might not be the best place for such things to be decided. The challenge of crime and punishment in a free society is unending.

Along with different viewpoints, "the fog of war" (adapted from a quote of former Secretary of Defense Robert McNamara) can certainly cause confusion in law enforcement. When self or a loved one is involved, it is hard to maintain objectivity. Perhaps fairness, in the long run, is just as important as legality. People must be treated with as much respect and dignity as they will allow. I have witnessed that even the police don't like to be policed very long.

Concerning crime and punishment, changes in strictness and leniency come and go. Often presented as new, the changes are usually promoted with a political agenda. At best they are adapted from a past experiment that may have been viewed as a failure then but is now presented as a likely success. The pendulum swings. It always will.

According to Ecclesiastes 1:9, 3000 years ago King Solomon said, "What has been will be again, what has been done will be done again; there is nothing new under the sun."

With the *Paths Crossed* series having now gone full circle, I will end it with the dedication it began with in *Villains-Victims-Victors:*

Dedicated to
the spouses and children of police officers.
They did not choose the profession,
but loved the person who did, and in doing so,
bore an untold burden.

DISCLAIMER

Paths Crossed – Heart Shots is creative <u>nonfiction</u>. In writing this book, the author has referenced many sources which are listed below. In resolving conflicts in information, the author defaulted to his training and experience as a detective to choose which information he felt most likely accurate. Few liberties have been taken in developing dialogue and such. The author is responsible for any errors or misinterpretations. Conjectures implied are those of the author.

SOURCES OF INFORMATION

Reports from the following sources:
    Michigan State Police report 42-1578-57 and 14-1439-13
    Indiana State Police report 11-11465
    Indiana Prison records of Victor Whitley
    A 75-Year History of the MSP by Phillip Schertzing
    Fallen Troopers of the MSP by Victor Beck
    Indiana State Police Newsletter of October 1957

Articles from the following newspapers:
    The Republic (10/01/57), Independent (10/02/57), Indianapolis Star (10/02/57, 06/25/82), The Brazil Daily Times (03/28/58), Dubois Daily Herald (10/05/57), North Vernon Plain Dealer (10/03/57, 10/17/57), North Vernon Sun (12/14/74, 02/17/79), The Evening News (10/01/57), Traverse City Record–Eagle (10/02/57), The Reporter (10/02/57), Seymour Daily Tribune (10/01-02-04-08-22/57, 11/01-02-11-16-18/57, 12/05/57, 03/25-28/58, 04/10/58, 06/28/00), The Daily Banner (03/28/58), The Scott County Journal (06/18/80), and Madera Tribune (10/01/57).

Stories from the following magazines:
Front Page Detective (JAN 1958)
True Detective Volume 68. Number 3 (JAN 1958)
Official Detective Volume XXVII, No. 1 (JAN 1958)

Interviews of the following persons:
KAY PELLOT ANDERSEN, widow of fallen Trooper
Dugald Pellot, whose amazing scrapbooks prompted the
author to recognize its potential as a book.
CHARLES WAGGONER, a retired ISP officer and attorney.
WARREN HUTCHINSON, a retired MSP officer and friend
of Trooper Dugald Pellot and Trooper Douglas Vogel.
TOM RICE, son of the late NVPD Police Chief Vernard Rice.
STEPHEN BERTRAM, stepson of Deputy Clyde Perkins.
GREG PELLOT, son of fallen Trooper Dugald Pellot.
ROBERT VOGEL, son of Trooper Douglas Vogel.
RICH KINSEY, a friend of Trooper Douglas Vogel.
MIKE KENENS, TERESA ASHER, and DONNA
WILSON, children of the Patrolman Lester Kenens.
BRIAN TAYLOR, grandson of Patrolman Lester Kenens.
JERRY SHARP, mortician that collected the body of Ralph
Taylor from the road and later buried him.
SANDRA TAYLOR, daughter-in-law of Ralph Taylor.
DAVID LEE, a retired ISP Officer and friend of fallen
Trooper Bill Kellems.
ERNEST WILSON, a retired ISP Officer who participated in
the manhunt that captured Victor Whitley.
GEORGE KERN, a retired ISP Officer whose late wife was
robbed by Ralph Taylor and Victor Whitley.
MELVIN RAY, a citizen who cared for Trooper Wm Kellems.
AL HOUGHTON, a retired MSP Detective Sergeant.
MICHAEL KNAUF, a past MSP Detective Sergeant.
LARRY ROTHMAN, an MSP Detective Sergeant.

ACKNOWLEDGEMENTS

Heart Shots, while the prequel to the *Paths Crossed* series, is the last book written in the series. A shocking, true story, it patiently waited 63 years to be told in detail and entirety. Kay Pellot Andersen is to be credited with bringing the events to the attention of this author. When the author began his research, things fell into place miraculously. It seemed the story could wait no longer and fate had chosen me to be its messenger.

First, allow me to salute the critical reviewers of this book: Darlene Staudacher, William Pelletier, Cindi Agge, Craig Medon, Warren Hutchinson, David Elwell, Charles Waggoner, and Nick Meier. They volunteered their precious time to critique the manuscript; their suggestions have been so valuable in making it better.

In addition to the aforementioned, the following persons made gracious and essential contributions to the creation of this book:

Sheila Kell, the genealogy specialist for the Jennings County Library, whose research was a significant contribution to this book. Bonita Welch, a volunteer at the Jennings County Library who donated vintage copies of detective magazines containing stories and pictures of the Taylor/Whitley crime wave.
Lauren Baker, ISP Museum Curator who enabled the author to connect with retired ISP members who knew Trooper Kellems.
First Sergeant Ron Galaviz, Indiana State Police.
Sergeant Carey Huls, Indiana State Police.
First Sergeant Bill Wibbels, Indiana State Police.
Archivist Michael Vetman, Indiana Archives & Records.
Jean Lee, a researcher at the Scott County Library.
Cindy Combs, a researcher at the Scott County Heritage Center.

Lynn Tolbert, son of ISP Detective Wayne Tolbert.
Marvin Richey, President of FOP#156, Scottsburg, Indiana.
Hans Andersen, whose insights and suggestions were helpful.
Jackie Burkhart, Ralph Taylor's granddaughter, who provided documents and pictures.
Michael O'Donnell, son of MSP Sergeant Fred O'Donnell.
John Southworth, son of MSP Detective Charlie Southworth.
Robert Muladore, author of *Tuebor, I will defend*.
Jim Driskill, Lenawee County (MI) Commissioner.

During the writing of this book, Kellie Adams of Socialbutterflybiz.net joined the Paths Crossed team as the Digital Marketing Coordinator. Her can-do attitude, timeliness, creativity, insight, and technical ability have been paramount to the successful launch of this project.

Deserving of a second mention is William Pelletier. He first served this project as a critical reviewer and then came aboard as the copy editor. As copy editor, he far exceeded the job description by challenging and coaching the author, and then bringing forward evidence the retired detective had missed.

To all mentioned above, and to my family who has supported me in this endeavor, and to anyone I have neglected to list, this author says, **"Thank you."**

AUTHOR BIOGRAPHY

Clif Edwards' professional life was as a lawman for 37 years. Few have experienced the diversity of his frontline law enforcement experiences and then written so vividly about them.

His police journey began at age 18, when he was recruited into the Michigan State Police. Nearly 27 years later, he retired at the rank of detective lieutenant.

A little over three months after retirement, 9/11 occurred. Like many Americans, Clif felt a call back to service and began working part-time as a Napoleon Township police officer. During that time period, he completed training to become a National Park Service protection ranger (federal law enforcement officer, emergency medical technician, wildland firefighter, search and rescue practitioner, and boat operator).

He then served 11 years as a protection ranger at three different marine wilderness national parks.

Clif now devotes his final years to writing while he explores North America, challenges himself with various outdoor activities, and volunteers on public lands. His sons and their families are his pride and joy.

PATHS CROSSED
Series

by
Clif Edwards

Book 1
VILLAINS - VICTIMS - VICTORS
Lessons Learned as a
Michigan State Police Trooper

Book 2
A CLOSER LOOK
Lessons Learned as a
Michigan State Police Detective Sergeant

Book 3
BATTLING DRUG DEALERS
Lessons Learned as a
Michigan State Police Detective Lieutenant

Book 4
PROTECTING NATIONAL PARKS
Lessons Learned as a
Law Enforcement Ranger

Prequel
HEART SHOTS
The Shocking True Story of a Dark Day in the
Michigan and Indiana State Police

Also
MISSOURI FARM GIRL ADVENTURES
A Children's Book

www.pathscrossed.info

Made in the USA
Monee, IL
15 December 2021

85487138R00095